PRAISE FOR *HOW TO*

'These 68 ideas aren't effortless. Not at all. They're effortful. They take work and it's worth it. Worth it because your lazy competitors are just standing by waiting for you to make a difference.'
Seth Godin – Author of *The Icarus Deception*

'An engaging, lively, and intensely practical guide to help put customer experience at the very centre of your business.'
Nick Chater – Professor of Behavioural Science, Warwick Business School and Co-Founder, Decision Technology Ltd

'If all you do is get one great idea from a book, the payoff is exponential. Well, here are 68 ideas that can help any company amaze their customers.'
Shep Hyken – *New York Times* Bestselling Author of *The Amazement Revolution*

'Truly lives up to its title. Packed with powerful, effective easy-to-implement tips that will transform your business into a genuine customer service champion.'
Dee Blick – FCIM Chartered Marketer and #1 Bestselling Marketing Author

'I love the way this book challenges management fads and lazy thinking and puts people at the heart of making businesses great.'
Guy Letts – Founder and CEO, CustomerSure

'Full of practical ideas that show you how to transform your business by standing in your customer's shoes. Adrian has given us a road map, now we need to act on it.'
Bernadette Jiwa – Brand Story Strategist and Bestselling Author

'Swinscoe offers practical, easy-to-implement tips on how to attract, engage and keep customers happy. Well worth reading.'
Steve Abernethy – Executive Chairman and Co-Founder, SquareTrade

'In *How to Wow*, Adrian has written a magnificent how to, based on interviews, data and his own down-to-earth knowledge of business. Drawing out the factors and attitudes that go into creating a fabulous customer experience, each of the 68 insights can be cherry-picked and you are bound to learn something.'
Minter Dial – President and Founder of The Myndset Company and Non-Executive Director at lastminute.com group

'This book will help you build a customer-centric culture that thrives! These 68 nuggets of customer service ideals will change the way you do business. Adrian presents actionable, practical concepts with examples, stories, and research. Highly recommended.'

S. Chris Edmonds – Speaker, Executive Consultant and Bestselling Author of *The Culture Engine*

'Adrian writes in a highly accessible and conversational manner that draws the reader in. The book has a clear focus on what it takes to deeply understand and continuously improve the customer journey experience. Ideas are well presented as being both challenging as well as opportunities to drive customer satisfaction. The 'How to Use It' and 'Insight in Action' sections are highly practical and this encourages the reader to take away ideas and apply them to real life situations. A handbook to dip in to for inspiration, it also is a potent reminder of just how important the small things as much as the big strategic initiatives.'

Beverly Landais – FCMI FCIM, Marketing and Business Development Director, Saunderson House, Wealth Management

'Finally! Adrian Swinscoe delivers a book jam-packed with 68 actionable concepts to increase both the customer experience and the employee experience. Beyond just theory, this book will benefit any business leader who wants to move the needle on customer service.'

Kevin Kruse – New York Times Bestselling Author of *Employee Engagement 2.0*

'As the informed and connected realm heightens every business' challenge to win and sustain customer share of mind, mastering customer experience emerges as the key lever. *How to Wow* offers a compendium of techniques deeply grounded in today's digital context. Consider culling a selection to fit your constituency or better yet, synthesising the whole into a timeless fabric that forms the core of success for any endeavour.'

Charlie Peters – Senior Executive Vice President, Emerson

'Essential and powerful insights for everyone who aspires to map out and enhance the customer journey and drive growth.'

Keith Lewis – COO, Matchtech Group plc

'If you are looking for a treasure chest of best practice and ideas in the customer experience field – *How to Wow* is just for you!'

Kevin Kelly, International Speaker and Best-Selling Author of *DO*!

'At a time when customers need to be treated better than ever before – their needs met, their complaints acknowledged and their whole selves engaged - Adrian Swinscoe gives a guideline to how businesses could improve. If customer service is at the heart of your business you would benefit from reading *How To Wow*.'

Will Beckett, Founder and CEO, Hawksmoor

'If you're looking to improve your customer experience, then there are 68 good reasons for you to read this book. With insights, tips and best next steps, this book ensures you will never be short of actions to drive up your customer satisfaction scores.'

Neil Davey, Editor, MyCustomer.com

'How to Wow simplifies the complexities of customer service into fundamental principles. Adrian's practical ideas can be easily implemented and will improve any business.'

Carey Smith, Founder and Chief Big Ass of Big Ass Fans

'Wish I'd had this book when I was starting my business! Invaluable guidance and so easy to access. Love the 'How to Use It' section.'

John Newton, Founder and Managing Director, The Ecology Consultancy

'We live in a world that is driven by the way interactions make us feel. Companies quickly learn that redesigning customer outcomes are not easy - Adrian Swinscoe has written a definitive guide to the re-invention of customer experience.'

Stewart M. Bloom, Chief Executive Officer, Aspect Software

'At last – a book that provides practical ways of delivering the superior experience that today's customers demand.'

Olivier Njamfa, Co-Founder and CEO of customer experience software company Eptica

'A 'go to' book for practical ideas for improving customer experience.'

Rob Brown, Director Customer Advocacy, Telstra

'Packed full of real-world examples and inspiration on every page, *How to Wow* is a priceless asset for leaders out to connect more deeply with team, customers - and their own values. I couldn't put it down, and you won't, either!'

Ted Coiné, CEO, OPENfor.business

'The lessons in Adrian's book are simple yet powerful. At the end of the day, it all comes back to earning customer trust, and his tips are important reminders for both leaders and those early in their careers.'

Peter Mühlmann, Founder and CEO, Trustpilot

'How to Wow is the ultimate guidebook for customer-obsessed companies and the leaders behind them. It's powered by two perspectives — both the customer's and the business's — that make it a must-read in today's age of the customer.'

Jim Dicso, President and CRO, SundaySky

'This is the only reference on customer experience use cases you will need to own. It is the fruition of the most in depth, ongoing collection of insights from the best practioners across the world. If you like to know all your bases are covered, this is the book to prioritise over all others.'

Martin Hill-Wilson, Customer Strategist, Brainfood Consulting

'I have enjoyed *How to Wow* in a way that I have not many others on the subject of customer experience. Adrian manages to coordinate the stories in such a logical way to lead the reader through the journey. An excellent read and a personal guide for anyone wanted to transform their organisation regardless of size.'

Damian Thompson, Director of Distribution, Principality Building Society

'*How to Wow* goes beyond providing 68 insights and instructions for creating a better customer experience. The book offers the facts and evidence to make the case to stakeholders as well as giving very clear instructions for those of us who are trying to implement a better customer experience in organisations.'

Melvin Brand Flu, Partner, Livework

'A great book crammed with simply articulated and well referenced insights, ideas and questions that will help anyone looking to improve their customer experience.'

Ryan Cheyne, People Director, Rentalcars.com

Adrian Swinscoe

HOW TO WOW

68 EFFORTLESS WAYS TO MAKE EVERY CUSTOMER EXPERIENCE AMAZING

PEARSON

Harlow, England • London • New York • Boston • San Francisco • Toronto • Sydney
Auckland • Singapore • Hong Kong • Tokyo • Seoul • Taipei • New Delhi
Cape Town • São Paulo • Mexico City • Madrid • Amsterdam • Munich • Paris • Milan

Pearson Education Limited
Edinburgh Gate
Harlow CM20 2JE
United Kingdom
Tel: +44 (0)1279 623623
Web: www.pearson.com/uk

First published 2016 (print and electronic)

ISBN: 978-1-292-11689-1 (print)
       978-1-292-11688-4 (PDF)
       978-1-292-11687-7 (ePub)

British Library Cataloguing-in-Publication Data
A catalogue record for the print edition is available from the British Library

Library of Congress Cataloging-in-Publication Data
A catalog record for the print edition is available from the Library of Congress

10 9 8 7 6 5 4 3 2
20 19 18 17 16

Cover design: Two Associates

Print edition typeset in Helvetica Neue LT W1G 9.5pt by SPi Global
Print edition printed in Great Britain by Henry Ling Ltd, at the Dorset Press, Dorchester, Dorset DT1 1HD

NOTE THAT ANY PAGE CROSS REFERENCES REFER TO THE PRINT EDITION

CONTENTS

PUBLISHER'S ACKNOWLEDGEMENTS

We are grateful to the following for permission to reproduce copyright material:

Figures

Figure 1.1 from Government Communication Service, Customer journey mapping [pdf], available at: https://gcs.civilservice.gov.uk/guidance/campaigns/customer-journey-mapping. Contains public sector information licensed under the Open Government Licence (OGL) v3.0. http://www.nationalarchives.gov.uk/doc/open-government-licence/version/3/.

Tables

Table on page 77 from Cabinet Office and Institute for Government (2010) MINDSPACE. Influencing Behaviour through Public Policy. London: Cabinet Office, page 8, © Crown Copyright 2012; Table on pages 78-9 after EAST: Four simple ways to apply behavioural insights, The Behavioural Insights Team, April 2014, Behavioural Insights Team, © Behavioural Insights Ltd 2014. Not to be reproduced, copied, distributed or published without the permission of Behavioural Insights Ltd; Table on pages 112-3 after Know Your Customer Service Persona, www.aspect.com/customer-service-personas, Aspect; Table on pages 135-6 after A client seminar called 'Delight from dissatisfaction', Mark Blackmore, Director of Lammore Consulting Ltd.

Text

Extract on page 61 from PLAIN (Plain Language Association InterNational).

ABOUT THE AUTHOR

Adrian Swinscoe is a consultant and adviser to a number of firms helping them improve their customer and client experience. His clients range from large publicly quoted organisations to fast-growing, entrepreneurial firms.

He's a huge fan of organisations that do great things for their customers and enjoys using research, stories and human insights to help create change and better results for his clients.

Overall, he's a lover of simplicity and an advocate of the human touch with some really useful technology thrown in.

Outside of work, he's a keen but distinctly average rock-climber and loves to develop and share ideas via his blog and his column on the Entrepreneurs section of **Forbes.com.**

You can learn more about Adrian at **www.adrianswinscoe.com**

INTRODUCTION

The British Museum in London has in its collection a customer service complaint letter[1] that is more than 3,700 years old. The letter, written on a clay tablet, originates from the Old Babylonian period (southern Mesopotamia) circa 1750 BC and is written by a man, Nanni, to a merchant, Ea-nasir. In the letter Nanni complains that there have been problems with two shipments of copper ore that he has ordered from the merchant. One was the wrong type and the other was delayed and delivered to the wrong location.

Different time. Familiar problems.

Now, whilst we don't know how Ea-nasir responded to Nanni, what we do know is that how we deliver great service and deal with our customers' problems has always been important.

However, in recent years we have seen the emergence of a new kid on the block . . . customer experience.

But, what is customer experience?

Definitions abound but I would describe it simply as 'the sum of all experiences that a customer has with a company'.

Moreover, it's come to the fore because as competition increases, customer behaviour and preferences change, and technology develops, the distinct differences between products and services are diminishing. Therefore, what we are left with and what can help companies distinguish themselves from their competitors is the service that they deliver to their customers and the overall customer experience that their customers have by interacting with them.

Customers are increasingly judging the companies they do business with on the customer experience they deliver. In 2011, research by Oracle[2] found that 89% of customers they surveyed reported that they had switched their business to a competitor following a poor customer experience. This was mirrored by research from American Express[3] in the same year, which found that the majority of customers around the world have abandoned or have not made a purchase because of poor customer service or a poor customer experience.

Moreover, Walker, a customer intelligence consulting firm, in another piece of research, found that it will become increasingly important and that, by 2020, customer experience will overtake price and product as the key brand differentiator in the business to business space.[4] Thus, customer experience is and will increasingly become a key competitive battleground; one that will define, at the very least, the first half of the 21st century.

Intuitively, most leaders, executives and entrepreneurs get this but because customer experience covers so many areas of their business they often struggle to define and articulate the Return on Investment (RoI) on new customer experience initiatives.

However, two recent studies help make the business case.

The first comes from Watermark Consulting[5] who in 2015 compared the stock returns from 2007 to 2013 of the top ten and the bottom ten ranked and publicly quoted companies in Forrester Research's annual Customer Experience Index.[6] What they found was that over this period, the top ten companies (the customer experience leaders) beat the performance of the overall S&P 500 Index by 35 points, whilst the bottom ten companies (the customer experience laggards) trailed the S&P 500 Index by 45 points. A difference of 80 points!

The second comes from Peter Kriss at Medallia who published an article in the *Harvard Business Review* called 'The Value of Customer Experience, Quantified'.[7] In it he explained about his research that aimed to quantify the value of delivering a good customer experience as opposed to a poor one and compared that across a couple of different types of business model. I was lucky enough to get a chance to speak to Peter and interview[8] him about his research. Here are the highlights of what he told me:

- His research compared two very different companies, each with over half a million customers. One operated a transactional business model and the other had a subscription based business model.
- He then looked at how much more their customers would spend if they had a great experience compared to if they had a poor experience.
- What he found from his research was that, in the case of the transactional business, spending by customers was 140% higher the following year after delivering a great customer experience versus a poor one.
- In the case of the subscription based business, customer retention went from 43% to 74% following a great customer experience versus a poor one.

So, having established the importance of customer experience and its business case the only thing to do now is to go off and deliver a great customer experience.

There are lots of books on customer experience and customer service that can help and many of them are good. But, in my opinion, many of them also contain lots of 'fluff' and all sorts of offers of the 'answer', e.g. if you follow our method you'll be assured of success.

The problem with that is that I don't believe there is one 'answer'. There is only what is right for your business and your customers and the problems that you face.

HOW THIS BOOK WORKS

As a result, this book aims to deliver a practical set of insights, tips and strategies based on what it takes to deliver a consistent, differentiated and world-class customer experience. The 68 insights are designed to be practical and easy to implement and are based on research, experience and over 150 interviews that I have conducted over the last 4–5 years with leading authors, entrepreneurs and customer service/experience experts and practitioners.

However, the insights and strategies are not meant to be an exhaustive set of strategies, neither are they applicable to every business. Rather, they are meant to be a 'Pick n Mix' range . . . you get to pick what you like and implement what works best for your business.

The insights are organised into a number of sections (see below) that both follow the customer lifecycle as well as addressing a number of internal dynamics and challenges that many businesses will have to face if they are to deliver their own great customer experience.

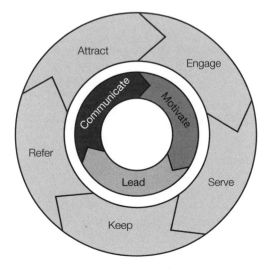

Whilst the insights are meant to stand alone, within each section I have tried to place them in a logical order that is aligned with the customer journey but also allows the insights to build on each other as the book develops.

Moreover, each insight is organised as follows:

1 An introduction – which lays out the insight and makes the case for it.
2 Insight in action – where a case study or an interview helps bring the insight to life and shows how it can be applied in practice.
3 How to use it – which takes the insight and suggests where to go next and what to do with this insight.

Finally, this book is less about channels, technology, systems and processes as many of these will change over time: it is more about relationships and people. People as customers and people that work inside organisations.

Enjoy.

PART 1

THE CUSTOMER PERSPECTIVE

SECTION 1

ATTRACT

INTRODUCTION

Attracting new customers is one of the hardest, if not the hardest, parts of being in business and with so much choice available to customers it's getting harder and harder.

Traditional advertising and marketing aims to use broadcast methods to raise awareness and attract attention. This, largely, talks 'at' customers. However, these days that is not enough as the majority of customers no longer believe what many businesses say about themselves. As a result, customers are doing more and more online and offline research about their buying decisions and are becoming ever more discerning about who they do business with and what they want. Therefore, it is not enough to create the 'coolest' new ad anymore and the size of your marketing budget is not always the best indicator of success. Rather, the best companies understand that in order to attract customers they have to engender their trust and be a company that customers believe can help them and that they want to be aligned with.

This section will share a number of insights, case studies, interviews and tips covering a range of issues surrounding a business's ability to attract new customers in the modern world including topics such as knowing where your customers start their journey, why it's essential for companies to be able to build trust at a distance, how the art of buying has changed and how companies need to respond to the changing behaviour of their customers.

INSIGHT 1 BE AT THE START OF YOUR CUSTOMER'S JOURNEY

Use this when you want to start attracting customers earlier in the buying process.

Prior to the internet, if we wanted to buy something new that we hadn't bought before then we would either look in a catalogue, talk to friends and family, go to a trade show, take a trip into the biggest local town or city – In my case, this was Edinburgh as I grew up in the Borders of Scotland and when I was young, this was a big deal – or wander down the street and talk to the owner of the local general store as they, at the time, seemed to know pretty much everything about everything.

This is how our buying journey used to start.

Nowadays, the way we buy is very different. For many people, one of the first things they do when they start thinking about buying something new is to go onto Google, Bing, Yahoo! or some other search engine and start finding out more about what they want, does it exist, who makes it, what do people think about it and what are the options, etc.

It might feel how we buy has fundamentally changed but, in reality, it hasn't. Yes, we have more information at our fingertips these days, but we're still looking for information, talking to people to find out more, looking for pointers of who to trust, who to talk to, where to find what we are looking for, etc.

Despite the sea changes that have happened over the last few years, it still surprises me that many businesses still think a customer's journey starts when he or she steps into their offices or shop, or at a first meeting. Those that do are missing a huge opportunity to connect with their customers at the start of their buying journey.

INSIGHT IN ACTION

As an example of a business sector that has gone through huge changes in recent years, let's look at the car industry, which according to a 2013 report from McKinsey[1] shows that:

- Traditionally, the average number of different dealers (whether new or used) that a customer would visit before buying was around five. This number has now fallen to as low as one dealer in some areas as more and more customers do their buying research online (over

80% of new-car and almost 100% of used-car customers) and make up their mind what sort of car they want before they even visit a car dealer.

- Whilst almost 90% of customers said that they would browse dealer websites or car manufacturer websites in the early stages of their buying and decision making journey, they would also use a variety of other online sources – manufacture and dealer websites, social media, blogs and forums – to gather information and compare offers.

Therefore, car dealerships can no longer rely on traditional methods of advertising and location to deliver the sales opportunities that they need to survive and thrive.

Successful players know that to thrive they need to put their customers' hat on and think about their journey. They need to understand that their customers' journey now starts before they get to the showroom and they need to provide answers to customers' questions via their website, their blog and on social media so that customers can find them. They know that they need to stop 'selling' and start helping and serving their customers. They know that one of the most powerful things that they can do is to display reviews and feedback from their recent customers as a way of building trust and confidence with their new customers. They also know that customers increasingly expect the retail experience to be seamless across channels – mobile, online, in-store.

HOW TO USE IT

Many customers are starting their buying journeys earlier and earlier and are conducting much of their buying research online. Firms need to realise this and work out how they can help their prospective customers with the early part of their buying journey.

To get started preparing to do that, here are some key questions for you to ask:

- Where does your customer's journey start?
- Are you there at the start of your customer's journey to help?
- What are they going to want to know around their purchasing decision, what are their fears, concerns, etc.?
- What's your niche or speciality? Do you want to be the best, the cheapest, the most trustworthy, the greenest, the most ethical, the

most of anything? Can you be that person? Can you display those qualities? And, it's not just about saying that you are the best, the cheapest, the most trustworthy, the greenest, the most ethical, the most of anything. You have to prove it.

■ Can social media tools like a Facebook page, a blog, a Twitter account, a LinkedIn group, an Instagram or Pinterest page help?

Answering these questions will give you some of the clues as to what you need to do to meet or, at least, be around your customers when they start their journey.

However, don't stop there. Once you've figured out what you need to do to make sure that you are there to help at the beginning of a customer's journey, keep going and map the rest of the customer journey. To help do that, you could use a customer journey map tool[2] like the one below:

Figure 1.1 Customer Journey Map Template

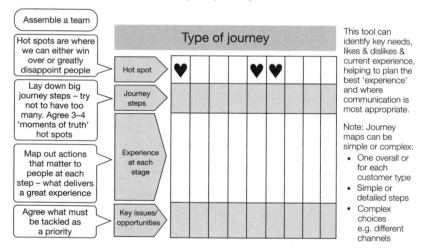

INSIGHT 2 DON'T INTERRUPT CUSTOMERS

Use this to save money and to stop annoying customers.

At a recent marketing conference I saw some statistics which claimed that:

- 86% of people skip ads on TV;
- 44% of direct mail is never opened;
- 91% of us unsubscribe to unsolicited marketing emails; and
- over 200 million people around the world are on 'do not call' lists.

These statistics are backed up by research in 2015 by Aimia Institute[3] which found that:

- 74% of UK customers state that they feel like they are receiving too many marketing emails and;
- 69% of UK customers have closed down customer accounts as a result of poorly targeted marketing campaigns.

It's not just a UK thing as research in 2015 by Marketo,[4] a marketing software firm, found that 63% of consumers across the US, UK, France, Germany and Australia expressed annoyance and frustration with brands that continue to bombard them with generic advertising messages and do so repeatedly.

What these findings suggest is that customers don't like to be interrupted and value their own time more than listening to a business's marketing message.

INSIGHT IN ACTION

How many adverts do we see every day? Hundreds? Thousands? How many do we remember?

How much junk mail do you get in the post? Have you ever faced the situation where a real letter has got lost or even thrown out with the junk mail?

Do you receive emails from companies that you have never done business with? Have you recently received a cold call from someone trying to sell you something and they just launch into their pitch without even asking if it's a good time to talk? Have you ever received an automated phone call trying to sell you something?

Have you done business with a company only to be added to their marketing list and then they start bombarding you with marketing offers and updates?

These are all interruptions and most of them don't work. Yet, the worst thing is that many companies ignore these signs and are wasting resources on ineffectual marketing campaigns and tactics.

Gary Vaynerchuk, a successful social media and wine entrepreneur as well as a sought after and entertaining speaker and best-selling author, sums up the situation very well and provides an alternative when he suggests that:[5]

- rather than spending $3 million on a Superbowl ad why not hire 60 people at $50k a year to deliver better service on Twitter or other social media channels or give this budget to an agency to deliver it for you; and

- most organisations are spending 20–30% of their money for no return.

HOW TO USE IT

Companies are still relying predominantly on traditional marketing methods to build awareness with customers and attract attention despite research that shows that customers think these are often ineffective. So, if your customers are not showing an interest in your marketing communications and you are not getting the responses that you want then review your marketing methods.

To help you get started, you should ask yourself some serious questions:

- Is your marketing targeted at the right people?
- Are you just trying to sell them something?
- Are you interrupting your customers more for your gain rather than theirs?
- Imagine what else you could be doing or investing in if you stopped wasting money on doing stuff that didn't work?
- What could you be doing that would help your customers rather than interrupt them?

Asking these questions will give you some clues about where you can save money and how you can stop annoying your existing customers.

INSIGHT 3 # DEVELOP TRUST AT A DISTANCE

Use this to help you understand how to let your customers get to know you better.

Many companies, large and small, cling on to the idea that they build trust with their customers when they get in touch, walk through the door, email them or pick up the phone.

However, research from Google and the Corporate Executive Board (CEB)[6] showed that business customers report that they are nearly 60% of the way through their buying journey before they get in touch with a company, regardless of how much the thing they are investigating costs. The same tends to be true of consumer purchases.

Successful companies and brands realise this and gear their website, blog, social media activity, digital marketing collateral and campaigns towards allowing customers to get to know them. They allow customers to get comfortable with them before they have even entered a shop, clicked on buy, called or emailed . . . something that has become known as content or inbound marketing.

INSIGHT IN ACTION

One company that is very good at this and helps other companies implement their own inbound marketing strategy with their software platform is Hubspot, the fast-growing and successful US software company.

Hubspot believe that because of the change in customer behaviour we are heading towards a world where inbound and content marketing may make up 80% of all marketing in the future.

In an interview[7] with Hubspot they also believe that:

- All businesses need to realise that the customer is now in control as they have the power to skip ads, screen out cold calls and filter out/ junk direct (e)mail.
- Doing so will also help them realise that they need to increase their inbound and content marketing efforts.
- Traditionally, most businesses have about 10% inbound and 90% traditional marketing in their mix.
- Hubspot's lead generation effort and spend is 75% inbound and content marketing, and 25% more traditional marketing. However, they think that an 80:20 split is probably the right ratio.

- Their inbound leads cost them half as much as leads from traditional marketing methods and they close customers at three times the rate of others.

HOW TO USE IT

Trust is earned and not given. This is just as true today as it's always been. However, developing trust with customers is becoming increasingly difficult given that many are making the majority of their buying decisions before they have even contacted a company. Firms need to respond and use tools like content and inbound marketing to help them build and develop trust at a distance.

To get started building your own 'trust at a distance' journey, you need to:

- Understand your buying personas. This means that when producing content, make sure whatever you create is targeted at the people you want to attract and engage. Hubspot started selling to two personas and now sell to six or seven.
- Successful inbound marketing = content + context. Your customer's lifecycle stage is your context. Your inbound marketing efforts will be even more effective if you are producing content that is right for your buying personas *but* is also aligned to where they are in their buying cycle, what jobs they want to accomplish and/or what decisions they need to make,[8] i.e. you need to be saying the right things to the right people at the right time.

NOTE

The biggest barrier to getting started with inbound and content marketing is fear – fear of doing something new and getting it wrong. Get over it and start. You will make mistakes but you will get better over time.

INSIGHT 4 ARE YOU BEING INTERESTING AND INTERESTED?

Use this to help you understand how to build better relationships with your customers.

It's a popular and often heard complaint amongst business leaders and marketers these days that it's getting harder and harder to generate awareness, attention and results from their marketing efforts.

However, one of the main problems is that many companies are still utilising traditional broadcast methods even in social channels to attract new customers and generate awareness. And that's where the problem lies.

Many businesses are still talking 'at' customers in an effort to be ever more interesting in the eyes of their customers. But, people have a limited appetite for being talked at.

This is playing out more and more in the business world and we are moving to an environment where relationships (and two-way, mutually beneficial, relationships) will drive future business growth. This is not a new concept but more of a back to basics approach to doing business, where you can grow your business through building better relationships with those around you. This idea was captured to great effect way back in 1936 by Dale Carnegie in *How to Win Friends and Influence People* when he said:

You can make more friends in two months by becoming interested in other people than you can in two years by trying to get other people interested in you.

INSIGHT IN ACTION

In reality, however, businesses need to strike a balance. Consider these two scenarios:

1 Imagine you are at a party or social function where you meet someone and all they do is talk about themselves. Beyond a certain point, it's quite natural that you'll become bored because all they are doing is talking about themselves. Right?

2 At the same party, imagine you meet another person and all they do is ask questions about you. There are two possible reactions here depending on your psychological and emotional state at the time.

You leave the conversation feeling like the person was a great friend and 'such a good listener' or you end up feeling like the continuous questioning ended up feeling a little 'creepy'.

These are two extreme examples, but they help to illustrate that the best and strongest relationships, whether in our personal lives or business, aside from things like trust and respect, tend to be built on two foundations:

- being interested; and
- being interesting.

What I mean is that you might have to be, or look interesting, or show an interest in someone or something to initiate or start a conversation. But, it will be the act of continually being interested in your customers or others that is equally important and responsible for maintaining the relationship.

HOW TO USE IT

Despite lots of data that many traditional marketing methods are, at best, not as effective as they were or, at worst, completely ineffective, many companies still persist and continue to talk 'at' their customers. However, to build sustainable relationships with your customers requires a different type of approach and one that combines both an 'interesting' and 'interested' approach.

To find out how you are doing with your marketing and if you are missing out on an opportunity to build better relationships with your customers, ask the following questions:

- What and how much in my marketing mix is trying to be interesting, to catch someone's attention, to get someone interested in me?
- What and how much in my marketing mix is focused on the interests of my customers, being interested in them, connecting with them and helping them?
- What's the balance between the two?

Asking these questions will give you some clues about where you may have gaps in your interesting and interested mix. In addition, using the answers to these questions, plot where you are on the following matrix and then develop a plan that maps out a path towards 'Best friend' status and a more balanced relationship.

Figure 4.1 The interesting and interested matrix

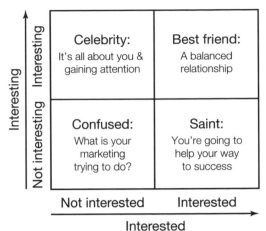

INSIGHT 5   TRUST DRIVES TRANSACTIONS

Use this to help you build up your trust levels in the minds of your customers.

In recent years we have seen big companies going bust through mis-management, a range of mis-selling scandals, financial crises, hacking and security breaches as well as a host of other things that have eroded our trust in the businesses around us.

In fact, according to the Edelman Trust Barometer,[9] which has been tracking trust in the business, government, media and non-governmental organisations (NGOs) for the last 15 years:

- less than 20% of us believe what companies say about themselves in their marketing and advertising; and
- academic, industry and company technical experts as well as our peers are seen as being twice as credible as company CEOs.

As a result, one of the key challenges for businesses in the 21st century is how do we develop, keep and nurture the trust of our customers.

Martha Rogers and Don Peppers[10] talk about this in their book *Extreme Trust* when they say that there is a new dynamic emerging where 'companies will be gauged on how they proactively protect the trust they have earned from their customers'.

INSIGHT IN ACTION

SquareTrade is a great example of a company that is leading the way on this issue. Not only are they one of the world's leading extended warranty service providers for consumer electronics and appliances but they are also developing exceptional levels of trust in an industry that has historically been distrusted and is low on service or transparency.

Steve Abernethy, Executive Chairman and Co-founder of SquareTrade, in an interview[11] explained that:

- The warranty industry has always been seen as a really crummy industry that lacked transparency and service.
- The warranty business was built around a model that minimised costs, made it hard for customers to claim and had no incentive to delight customers.

- Therefore, SquareTrade:
  - Made their service transparent and researchable so that consumers could research their warranty products and find out what other customers were saying about them.
  - Made their claim process a branding and service experience exercise and not a cost-minimisation experience.
- Their objective was to create a customer for life and not just worry about profiting from one warranty.
- Their results and reviews speak for themselves. Currently they have an Apple App Store average score of 4.5 out of 5 based on 7000+ reviews, a 4.7 out of 5 average score based on 35,000+ reviews on Amazon and a 4.9 out of 5 average score on 600+ Google reviews.

HOW TO USE IT

Increasingly, customers are looking to reviews and customer feedback whether on company websites or third-party sites as a way of evaluating if they would like to do business with that company. Some companies still resist this as they get hung up on what happens when they get a negative review rather than focusing on when things go right.

Compare that resistance with research findings from Trustpilot, an open, review-driven community connecting online consumers. According to their former Chief Marketing Officer, Jan Jensen, their research shows that: 'Displaying "earned" trust scores can help improve conversion rates by up to 58%.'[12]

So, if you believe in what you are doing, if you believe in the quality of the product and/or service you provide and want to compete in the modern marketplace then there are two things that you have to do:

1 Start asking your customers for feedback and reviews.

2 Start displaying your reviews on your website and social channels.

Your customers are going to talk about you anyway. But, by gathering and displaying your reviews you can have some influence in that conversation.

INSIGHT 6   BECOME PART OF YOUR CUSTOMER'S STORY

Use this to help you build meaning in the mind of a customer.

These days businesses are having trouble attracting and keeping the attention of their customers. The ones that do successfully hold people's attention tend to be those that have a brand story that has meaning in the minds of their customers.

Bernadette Jiwa in her book *The Fortune Cookie Principle* explains[13] it very well when she says that:

> Every product or service has two elements to it: The cookie (the commodity part of it) and the fortune (the meaning that we attach to it).

People don't buy things, they buy how it makes them feel.

Moreover, Jeremy Waite[14] in his 2015 book *From Survival to Significance* believes that there is an emerging space for brands that become significant. Significant to their customers, their marketplace, their community, the world. In his book Jeremy quotes Simon Sinek, the best-selling author of *Start With Why*, who says:

> The goal in business is not to sell to people who need what you have, it is to do business with people who believe what you believe.

Significance, therefore, is not significance to everyone but significance to some.

INSIGHT IN ACTION

Successful businesses make their purpose their customers and what they care about; they make them the 'heroes' of their story.

GOOD EXAMPLES

TOMS, a shoe company, has grown phenomenally quickly based on a simple idea of 'One For One' where they donate one pair of shoes to children in need for every pair that they sell. Since they were founded in 2006 by Blake Mycoskie, they have given away more than 45 million pairs of new shoes[15] and they have now extended their business and giving model into eyeware/glasses.

Patagonia, an outdoor clothing and equipment company, has pioneered conscious consumption amongst its customers based on its values and concern for the environment.

Hiut Denim, a jean manufacturer, was established by David Hieatt to try and revive Cardigan, where they are based, as it used to be Britain's largest producer of jeans, producing 35,000 pairs of jeans a week for 30–40 years.[16] Jeans are the uniform for creative people and David spent his working life with creative people and their ideas always inspired him. So, with the Hiut Denim Company, he set out 'to make a great product, in a great town that knows how to make that great product and sell it to those great people'.

HOW TO USE IT

Customers are increasingly choosing and aligning themselves with companies they feel an affinity towards, whether that is based on a set of shared values or a shared purpose.

This is not business as usual for many firms and so to start building your brand or company story, you have to start with figuring out what business you are actually in. To do that, you need to begin with the end in mind. However, it's not your end, where you talk in terms of profits and sales; instead you have to figure out your customers' end.

Answering these questions will help you get started with that process:

- When your customers buy your product or service how do they feel?
- Compare that to how you want to make them feel?
- What does your company stand for?
- What is your company's purpose?
- Does what you stand for or your purpose make a difference to the lives of your customers?
- What do your customers care about?
- How can you align your purpose with what your customers care about?

INSIGHT 7 CUSTOMER BEHAVIOUR IS CHANGING: CHECK YOUR ASSUMPTIONS

Use this to make sure that you are not making the wrong sort of assumptions about your customers.

When we set out to design, build and deliver a great customer experience – or anything else for that matter – we tend to make assumptions about who it is for, what they like, what they prefer and what they enjoy.

However, in the face of ever-changing consumer behaviour, can we be sure that our assumptions are correct?

A quote from Alan Alda, the famous actor, offers some sage advice:[17]

Your assumptions are your windows on the world. Scrub them off every once in a while or the light won't come in.

INSIGHT IN ACTION

Here's an example of a popular assumption that many of us make and a possible, alternative, explanation.

Assumption: Our attention spans are getting shorter

The US National Center for Biotechnology Information[18] reports that our attention span has decreased from 12 seconds in 2000 to 8 seconds in 2014.

However, other reports put the average attention span of a goldfish at 9 seconds!

But, if our attention span is getting shorter then would it not follow that things like films should be getting shorter too?

That's where we face a problem as, in fact, the opposite is true. Films over the last two decades have got longer.[19] The five highest-grossing films of 2014 had an average length of 142 minutes up from an average length of 118 minutes in 1992 for the five highest-grossing films of that year.

In actual fact, what seems to be happening is that although our attention span feels like it is getting shorter, in reality, we are becoming more and more dismissive of things that don't interest or engage us, or are not valuable, helpful or relevant to us.

HOW TO USE IT

Customer behaviour is changing and old assumptions about what different demographic groups like, do or prefer are not as valid as they once were. Therefore, companies need to be careful about the assumptions that they make about their customers.

This has implications for the design and delivery of customer experience. To understand how, here are a few things that you should do:

- Be clear about the assumptions that you are making about your product or service and your target market.
- Make your assumptions explicit and list them out.
- Then, go and check them against what your customers actually do, think and value.

You might be surprised what you find out.

INSIGHT 8 DATA INSIGHTS ARE GOOD BUT IMMERSION AND OBSERVATION ARE BETTER

Use this when you need to get to know your customers better.

The business press is awash with stories of the promise and possibilities of 'big data' and what we can learn from the huge amount of data that exists about our customers not just within our company walls but also on the internet and in social media.

But, we need to remember that data is only data however big it is and it is analysis that identifies trends, groupings and statistically significant events. Therefore, it's important to remember that 'big data' is just that . . . lots of data . . . and the thing that counts is what we do with the data.

While big data insight into customers' behaviour can be good, sometimes the answers are right in front of you . . . and more often than not they are in the hands of your customers.

As Dave Carroll of *United Breaks Guitars* video fame says:[19]

> *There are no statistically insignificant portions of your customer base anymore.*

Big data insight into customers' behaviour can be good but often immersion and observation are better.

INSIGHT IN ACTION

A great example of this comes from Sir Terry Leahy, former CEO of Tesco, who is widely credited with turning Tesco's from Britain's third biggest supermarket into the world's fourth biggest food retailer in just over a decade.[20] Prior to stepping down in 2010, he was a great fan of spending time talking to and observing customers. In fact, he reputedly spent up to 40% of his time talking to customers and in store.

Commentators have suggested[21] that his successors deviated from this type of approach and leadership and this, in a large part, led to many of Tesco's problems in 2014 and 2015.

Imagine the sort of insight that you could develop if you adopted Leahy's approach on a regular basis? Moreover, imagine the impact on your customers and your staff if you kept showing up.

The *Financial Times* in 2010[22] wrote about the impact on Tesco's staff:

Sir Terry conveyed a sense of direction to his workforce and convinced them – by the amount of time he spent on the shop floor and listening to customers – that he understood people's jobs and cared about what they were doing.

HOW TO USE IT

In 1931, Alfred Korzybski, the Polish American scientist and philosopher, famously remarked that 'the map is not the territory'. What he meant is that people often confuse models of reality with reality itself. The same can be said of data and insights from data about customers . . . they are only representations of reality. They can be useful but we should be careful not to rely solely on them. We should also spare a little time for the human insights that can be gained by spending more time as a customer of your own business and with, and observing, your customers.

If you want to boost your own personal insight into your customers then allocate more time to:

- being your own customer;
- serving your own customers;
- talking, listening and learning from the people that serve your customers;
- watching your customers in real time in your own business; and
- watching your customers interact and transact in real time with other businesses.

Do that and you'll get real and practical insights much faster than you would get using any other method. Yes, you could contract that out to an agency to conduct a mystery shopping exercise and you could delegate it to one of your team to do. But, beware. Do that and you'll lose the emotional insight that you'll get from also doing it yourself.

SECTION 2

ENGAGE

INTRODUCTION

Many companies as soon as they attract some attention from potential new customers switch straight into 'sales' mode. That may be OK if you are dealing with a one-off, low-value transaction but it's not a great strategy if you want to build a longer-lasting relationship as more often than not it just pushes customers away. Customers don't want to be sold to. Therefore, to build a longer lasting relationship, one that focuses on value, engagement and loyalty, requires a different approach. It will have to be one that is more open, generous and has a greater degree of empathy with a customer's needs. To build that sort of relationship requires understanding yourself and the sort of relationship you currently have with your customers, what it is going to take to develop those relationships and what it means to build trust.

This section will attempt to provide some insights into a range of issues surrounding what it takes to engage customers in the modern world. As such, it will cover topics such as why you need to really understand and be honest about the sort of relationships that you have with your customers, what it takes to build trust, how to be more interesting to your customers, why everything you do matters to your customers, all the way through to the importance of empathy and generosity in the engagement process.

UNDERSTAND THE RELATIONSHIPS YOU HAVE WITH YOUR CUSTOMERS

Use this to help categorise the relationships that you have with your customers and understand how you can better manage and develop them.

There are various types of relationships that a customer can have with a business. These can range from being purely transactional, where the customer knows what they want, they come, they buy, they leave . . . all the way through to a partnership arrangement, where the customer and the business act as one.

In today's modern world, in order to manage and grow your customer relationships you have to understand what type of relationship you have with your customer, how this has changed over time, what sort of relationship they would like to have with you and the sort of relationship you want to build with them. You should do this before you do anything.

INSIGHT IN ACTION

Imagine if we applied the typology of personal relationships to help us categorise our customer relationships? Would that help us better understand our customer relationships, where we stand with our customers and how we can develop the relationship?

How about a customer relationship typology that goes something like this:

Type or stage of relationship	Description
Dating	Your customers are transient, they like variety and choice but they don't want an exclusive relationship. An alternative explanation is that they know what they are looking for but they haven't found the business or brand that they want to have an exclusive relationship with yet. They are shoppers and they may come back but don't count on it. And, if they do, you may have to offer them great deals or discounts to keep them coming back.

Type or stage of relationship	Description
One night stand	You've been able to deliver a one-off experience to your customers but they don't want more. Their business could have been an impulse purchase or be driven by a specific need or context. These customers offer little prospect of repeat business.
Boyfriend or girlfriend	Your customers and you know each other, like each other and are getting to know each other better. You're loyal to each other, you have an exclusive relationship, you both get benefits out of it and are excited about getting to know each other better.
Engaged	You've fallen in love with your customers and they've fallen in love with you. So much so, that you are committed to each other and are planning on building a future together. You're looking forward to signing contracts and embarking on a new partnership together.
Married	You are now really connected. This would involve exclusive offers, membership packages, loyalty programmes, priority service, special surprises, etc. . . . the whole 9 yards. Contracts and vows are exchanged. In fact, the relationship may, in time, produce new ventures and investments, etc. However, don't take the relationship for granted. Terminating or breaching terms of contracts can be messy.
Partner	This is like being married but is slightly less formal and without any contracts. However, it doesn't imply any less commitment, love or loyalty. But, also like marriage, the absence of contracts, doesn't necessarily mean that breaking up is any less messy.

HOW TO USE IT

Businesses must realise that the relationships they have with their customers differ across the customer lifecycle and are dependent on the type of business. To help with that they should categorise the relationships they have with their customers so that they can better understand them and then manage and develop them. However, businesses need to be honest and realistic in their assessment, as former CEO of first direct, Mark Mullen, puts it when he says:[1]

> *As a business you have to understand the limits of customer interest in your business.*

So, if you want to build your levels of engagement with your customers, here's what you should do next:

1 Conduct an honest audit of the relationships that you have with your customers.

2 Plan out what sort of relationships you would like to have.

3 Give this a reality check against the interests of your customers.

4 Review your plan based on your reality check.

5 Design your marketing, engagement, community and service efforts with your relationship goals in mind.

6 Review on a regular basis (relationships are dynamic and will change over time).

INSIGHT 10   WHAT IT TAKES TO BUILD TRUST

Use this to help you build a company that is more trusted by its customers.

What is trust? Well, according to the *Oxford Dictionary,* trust is defined as having a:

Firm belief in the reliability, truth, or ability of someone or something.

Martha Rogers and Don Peppers, authors of a book called *Extreme Trust,* believe that there is a new dynamic emerging where companies are now being gauged by their customers on how they proactively protect the trust they have earned from their customers.

They go on to say that to build trust with customers businesses need to do three things:

1 do things right;

2 do the right things; and

3 be proactive.

However, it's the third element that's the crucial one here as it's no longer good enough to just be good enough. Now, you have to be proactive in showing and proving that you can be trusted. Businesses can no longer afford to take their customers' trust for granted. They have to earn it and keep earning it. Charlie Peters, Senior Executive Vice President of Emerson, a diversified global manufacturing and technology company, concurs[2] with this and believes that a firm's 'competitive advantage will be built and maintained on its ability to build trust'.

INSIGHT IN ACTION

Martha Rogers and Don Peppers, in an interview,[3] go on to cite Amazon as a great example of a firm that does a great job of developing a trusted relationship with their customers by helping them make additional buying decisions via their product recommendations, which are based on the customer's buying history. They then follow that up with user reviews and recommendations of complementary products. Moreover, in their quest to keep building the trust levels that they have with their customers, they will alert you if you have bought, for example, the same book before and will check with you to make sure that you are not making a mistake in purchasing another copy.

HOW TO USE IT

We all know that trust is hard to earn but very easy to lose.

We also know that these days businesses are trusted for how they are and what they do much more than any fancy exterior or perfectly crafted message.

Therefore, building trust can start simply with some back to basics relationship-building principles like:

1 Be more courteous and polite towards everyone.
2 Treat and give everyone your respect.
3 Do the things that you say you will do when you say you will do them.
4 Give before you receive.
5 Be honest.
6 Be open.

However, to really put this into action and start generating results, consider developing a scorecard or measurement system to keep track of how you are doing on these sort of trust building behaviours and where you can improve.

INSIGHT 11 # CUSTOMERS TRUST PEOPLE LIKE THEM

Use this to get your customers to help you build a more trusted brand.

Earlier in the book, I mentioned that according to the Edelman Trust Barometer[4] 'less than 20% of us believe what companies say about themselves in their marketing and advertising'. Moreover, the report goes on to say that 'experts' and 'a person like yourself' are seen as being twice as credible as CEOs.

This is particularly true in online commerce where businesses are often not trusted and customers, around the point of purchase, don't always have access to trusted advice when making purchases.

Leading firms understand this and utilise 'experts' like academics, industry experts or their very own technical experts to help with their customer engagement. Others leverage the 'a person like yourself' opportunity and utilise their own and existing customers to help them engage new customers.

INSIGHT IN ACTION

One innovative approach to the 'a person like yourself' challenge comes from Scott Pulsipher, President and COO of Needle, a US software firm that is pioneering advocate-assisted commerce. In an interview,[5] Scott explains how:

- Needle helped Carhartt, who provide technical workwear, find and engage their advocates so that when a Carhartt shopper is displaying certain behaviours on the website, the shopper will get an invite (pop-up) that asks them if they would like to 'chat' with a Carhartt 'expert' customer who may be able to help them with any purchasing questions they have.

- All of the advocates are clearly identified through their bios and pictures as fans of the company, experts and purchasers of the company's products.

- If the customer clicks yes then this tends to lead to a dramatic increase in the customer being able to locate the right product, higher customer satisfaction and net promoter scores as well as higher and more frequent purchases.

- Moreover, this approach can lead to a 6–10 fold increase in conversion over a self-service customer and a 10–25% increase in the average order value.

HOW TO USE IT

Research suggests that customers trust people that are similar to them, technical and/or industry experts more than they do the firms that they do business with.

Firms need to leverage these insights and build trust with their customers. To do so, consider following the example of leading firms and make sure that:

- The technical experts within your firm are just as accessible to your customers as your sales people are.
- You utilise industry and academic experts as much as possible when it comes to reviewing your products and services.
- You introduce your new customers to your existing customers as much as possible so that they can hear directly from them regarding what your product and service is really like.

INSIGHT 12 — TO REALLY ENGAGE YOU MUST BE WILLING TO FAIL

Use this to help you understand that customers often don't mind failures when they trust your brand.

Too often we encounter situations where people don't do things or try things because they are afraid to fail.

Trusted brands with engaged customers, however, will have tried and failed a number of times

Just look at Apple and the number of times that they have launched things that haven't worked.[6] Remember the Apple Lisa or the U2 iPod? Yes? No?

To engage your customers and to keep them engaged you must be willing to try new things and, in doing so, you must be willing to fail.

INSIGHT IN ACTION

An excellent example of this idea in action comes from Seth Godin, the bestselling author.

Back in 2012 he wrote a book called *The Icarus Deception,* which was about how, in the modern and connected world, we need more and more people to create 'Art'. When Seth uses the word 'Art' he is not referring to anything to do with decoration or painting but, rather, things that connect with other people and make change happen.

However, when it came to *The Icarus Deception* rather than working with a traditional publisher to develop and release the book as he had done with a number of the other books that he has published, he organised a Kickstarter appeal to get the project funded.

This was a huge risk, especially for a well-known author, as it had never been done before and not getting the book funded would have been a very public failure.

The project, however, did get funded and reached its target of $40,000 in around 3 hours! Overall, the project generated 4,242 backers at various levels who funded it to the tune of $287,342. I'm proud to say I was one of the backers.

IN AN INTERVIEW WITH SETH,[7] WHEN DISCUSSING THE BOOK PROJECT HE TOLD ME THAT:

You can't make 'Art' if you are not willing to fail.

The cost of failing these days is incredibly low and the main reason that prevents people from trying is fear.

We are taught that when the stakes are high we should back off. But what *The Icarus Deception* argues is that when the stakes are high, backing off is the worst thing that we could possibly do.

HOW TO USE IT

Customers want and expect the brands that they trust to innovate and experiment as they continue to deliver value. They also understand that not all innovations will work but their trust in the brand is strong enough to survive and prosper beyond these failures.

Therefore, to maintain and grow the trust and engagement that you have with your customers you must be willing to innovate, experiment and, in the worst case scenario, fail.

The key here is to innovate and experiment in an environment or culture that allows failure, where experimentation in a small way is allowed, where failure is not fatal for the business or anyone's career and where you can, through your failures, learn how to start doing innovative or unique work. Once you have found or created that environment or culture you will be well on your way.

But, it's important to remember to start small as it's only after you have tried to do new things in a small way that you will earn the right to do them in a larger way.

Now, go try something that might fail. It's the best way to be innovative and the best way to learn.

DOING WHAT'S RIGHT FOR THE CUSTOMER IS OFTEN AN ARTICLE OF FAITH

Use this to help you understand or show that doing the right thing for the customer sometimes runs counter to what your economic or financial calculations tell you.

Business is full of calculations and numbers. Budgets, forecasts, profit and loss statements, operational analysis, investment decisions, business cases, return on investment calculations, etc. As a result, decisions to do, or not to do, something are often dominated by financial, economic and, ultimately, rational decision making.

But, when it comes to innovating around customer relationships and increasing engagement it can be difficult to directly quantify the financial and economic returns of something that is primarily emotional in nature.

As a result, many firms, won't proceed, won't innovate, won't take risks, won't 'do the right thing' by their customers because they can't make the business case for that action.

However, just because you cannot make the financial business case for doing something doesn't necessarily mean that you shouldn't do it. Voltaire had an interesting perspective on this when he said:

> To be absolutely certain about something, one must know everything or nothing about it.

Sometimes you have to be prepared to make a leap of faith.

INSIGHT IN ACTION

A great example of this type of approach comes from Amazon. Now, Amazon are an extremely smart, sophisticated and innovative technology business and they use data analysis, science, mathematics and economics extensively when they are running and developing their business. However, in an interview with *Harvard Business Review*,[8] Amazon's CEO Jeff Bezos offers some very interesting and additional insights into how they do business:

> When things get complicated, we simplify by saying, what's best for the customer? And then we take it as an article of faith if we do that that it'll work out in the long term. So, we can never prove that. In fact,

sometimes we've done price elasticity studies, and the answer is always we should raise prices. And, we don't do that because we believe – and again, we have to take this as an article of faith – we believe by keeping our prices very, very low, we earn trust with customers over time, and that that actually does maximize free cash flow over the long term.

What's really interesting about this is that despite extensive use of technology, economics, financial and data analysis techniques, Amazon understand that these tools can only take them so far and that sometimes they can stop you doing things that are in the best interests of customers.

As a result, Amazon know that if they are to build better relations with their customers, they often have to do what they believe and feel is right for their customers and ignore what their calculations are telling them.

HOW TO USE IT

Doing the right thing for the customer is not always supported by standard economic or financial calculations and sometimes needs to rely on a 'gut' feeling or a leap of faith.

To help you understand how much of your decision making is driven by economic and financial calculations and where you may be missing an opportunity, ask yourself these questions:

- How many customer-related initiatives have you stopped lately?
- How many of them have you stopped or not started purely on economic or financial grounds?
- How many of them could have helped you improve engagement with your customers but you couldn't make the business case for them?
- How many of those could you describe as 'doing the right thing'?
- Should you go back and review some of your decisions given the case that is being made for 'doing the right thing'?
- Is there something that, in future, you could do differently that will allow you to include an element of 'doing the right thing' in how you deliver your customer service and experience?

INSIGHT 14 HOW TO BE MORE INTERESTING

Use this to help you become more interesting, relevant and engaging to your customers.

Competition to win the attention of customers is intense and is increasing. However, too often businesses seek to win the attention of customers by trying to outspend and make more 'noise' than their competitors.

But, more doesn't always cut through the 'noise'. More might grab someone's attention for a while but there is no guarantee that it will necessarily sustain it.

Taking the time and putting the effort into making yourself more interesting and more relevant to your customers, however, can be a unique differentiator.

Like in life, if you make your business more interesting to your customers then you'll get talked about, get shared and are more likely to get the attention, engagement, sales and loyalty that you desire.

Interesting stands out.

INSIGHT IN ACTION

Jessica Hagy, the artist and best-selling author who is widely known for her award winning blog, Indexed,[9] tackled this subject in an article she wrote in 2011 for Forbes on 'How To Be More Interesting (In 10 Simple Steps)'.[10] That article was incredibly popular and has been read over 2 million times. Since then she has expanded it into a book: *How to Be Interesting: An Instruction Manual*.

In an interview with Jessica,[11] she explained that there are ten habits and behaviours that you can develop to make yourself or your business more interesting.

TEN HABITS

Go exploring: Be curious and seek out new ideas, places and opinions.

Share what you discover: Not everyone will see or experience what you have so share what you have found with others.

Do something, anything: Something that is active is much more interesting and positive than something that isn't.

Embrace your innate weirdness: Don't try to be like everyone else and hide what makes you different. Find your difference and celebrate it.

Have a cause: People love a business that is trying to do more and be more, particularly, when it's not just about making more money.

Minimise the swagger: Ego and arrogance cloud people's ability to see expertise.

Give it a shot: Try something. It might not work. But, if you've never failed then you've never really learned anything.

Hop off the bandwagon: Bandwagons are for followers. Is that what you are? I thought you wanted to be a leader.

Grow a pair: Doing something different takes courage and involves a bit of risk. Would you rather talk about that business or be that business that is talked about?

Ignore the scolds: Some people will always warn you against deviating from the norm or try and drag you down. Ignore them. That's their fear, don't let them make it yours.

HOW TO USE IT

Being interesting is a core element of any relationship and, in a business sense, is a real driver of differentiation, attention, engagement, sales and advocacy.

However, being or becoming more interesting doesn't always happen by accident and needs to be worked on. To make themselves more interesting to their customers, firms need to adopt different behaviours.

Jessica has provided some great advice on areas where you can make yourself more interesting. Start by being more curious and go exploring. That will help you find different ideas to help you develop new ways of doing things and thinking about the way you do them.

Do that and you'll become more interesting.

However, if you find that hard, then start small and start with one thing. But, make sure you start.

For example, pick one habit from the list above, start thinking about it, start working on it and you'll soon start to reap the benefits.

INSIGHT 15   # EMPATHY IS KEY TO ENGAGEMENT

Use this when you want to build understanding, empathy and really figure out what it's like to 'walk a mile' in your customer's shoes.

A common definition of empathy is being able to 'walk a mile in someone else's shoes'. According to the *Oxford Dictionary,* it is also defined as:

The ability to understand and share the feelings of another.

Fundamentally, empathy is a skill and like any other skill it can be learnt and we can all get better at it. Working on building empathy into your business and your team can have huge implications for customer engagement, employee engagement, leadership, customer service, marketing, change, culture, etc.

However, many firms struggle with building real empathy with their customers (and their employees).

HERE'S WHERE AND WHY SOME FIRMS ARE FAILING

They pay little attention to their customers' perspective as they are more focused on their own products and services and, therefore, are disconnected from their customers; or they struggle to understand why what they are doing is not working as well as it could do.

They are not generous with their time, effort, care or resources towards their people and their customers and, so, wonder why when they ask for their help they get little in return.

They might have insight but unless they show it or demonstrate it nothing happens or gets done.

Empathy is the basis of a deep and meaningful closeness in a relationship and is the foundation of the experience of 'we' rather than just 'I' or 'you'. If your customer senses that you really feel how it is for them, they will start to feel less anxious and stressed, becoming closer and more trusting.

INSIGHT IN ACTION

But, how can a firm build and show empathy in practice?

One really interesting example comes from Siemens Industry Automation and Drive Technologies, that I encountered while I was a judge at the UK Customer Experience Awards[12] a couple of years ago.

Their business focuses on developing solutions to help their clients improve operational efficiency, energy management and enhance the safety of manufacturing plants. To drive empathy in their business and improve their customer's experience, they routinely 'embed' a member of their team within a customer's business for a fixed period of time or on a regular basis. Doing so gives them incredible insight into their customer's business, what is important to them, what is a challenge and how Siemens can change, add or improve their service to serve them better.

HOW TO USE IT

To really engage your customers requires that you understand them, their hopes, desires and fears. That requires empathy and to acquire that can often take time and hard work.

A key way to do this is to spend time with your customers, listening to them and seeing things through their eyes. To do this, Siemens embeds a member of their team into their customer's business. However, depending on your business, this may not always be possible or the easiest thing to do.

To start building your empathy and greater engagement with your customers, ask the following questions:

- How can we emulate Siemens?
- How can we spend more time with our customers, listening to them and seeing things through their eyes?
- How can we help our people walk a mile in our customers' shoes?

Doing so will help you gain a higher degree of empathy and insight that will pay huge dividends.

INSIGHT 16

BAD CORPORATE BEHAVIOUR IMPACTS CUSTOMER EXPERIENCE AND ENGAGEMENT

Use this to understand the impact that everyone's behaviour has on your customer experience.

A business's ability to engage and build trust with its customers is not just dependent on how its employees treat or serve their customers. It can also be affected by what a company does as part of its strategy, what it stands for as well as the actions of its executives.

INSIGHT IN ACTION

EXAMPLES OF FIRMS LOSING CUSTOMER ENGAGEMENT

In 2013, many of the large UK energy firms put up their prices by, on average, 9% for both gas and electricity. This caused a huge amount of uproar and concern amongst consumers, particularly as inflation was currently running at around 2.5%, the announcements were made at the beginning of winter and many people in the UK were facing 'fuel poverty'. Following the announcements, a story in the *Evening Standard*[13] reported that complaints had surged at large energy firms in the UK.

Again in 2013, Paul Flowers, the Co-operative Bank's former chairman, was arrested in connection with the supply of illegal drugs. He was then removed from his post. Subsequently, Nunwood's Customer Experience Excellence Centre[14] released a report which showed that The Co-operative Bank had dropped out of the UK's top 100 firms, when it comes to the delivery of customer experience. In the previous year, they had earned a position of 26 out of 100. Customer service or experience is heavily dependent on perception. Therefore, it is reasonable to assume that the behaviour of Paul Flowers had a large and negative impact on the perception of the bank and played a significant role in the Co-operative Bank's fall down the rankings.

Similarly, Amazon and Starbucks in the UK suffered negative effects on their customer experience rankings over the course of 2013 as a result of a number of stories about their accounting policies and how much UK corporation tax they pay. According to the Nunwood report, Amazon fell to 4 in the rankings after three years at number 1, whilst Starbucks, like the Co-operative Bank, dropped out of the top 100.

2013 wasn't an isolated year and these examples can be found, not only in the UK, but year after year across the world.[15] Moreover, the UK's Ombudsman's Service released a report in early 2015 entitled the Consumer Action Monitor,[16] which found that complaints about products or services made in 2014 were almost double the number made in 2013. However, one of the most important and interesting findings of the report was an increasing cynicism amongst customers about company motives, with 33% of consumers reporting that they believe big businesses are only interested in money.

HOW TO USE IT

A large part of a customer's experience is perception. Perception of how good or usable your website is, how friendly your staff are, how ethical your firm's policies and procedures are or how your leaders behave in and out of the office. However, many firms overlook the latter two issues and their impact on the customer experience.

To better understand how your corporate behaviour and that of your leaders is affecting your ability to engage your customers and build trust with them, ask yourself the following questions:

- How does your strategy fit with the expectations of your customers?
- How do you know?
- Your employees and executives are ambassadors for your company, how good a job are they doing?
- How do you know?
- Is your firm getting talked about for something other than its products, services and quality of its customer experience?
- Is the talk negative and critical?
- What have you done to deserve this criticism?
- What are you going to do about it?

INNOVATING AROUND RELATIONSHIPS

Use this to evaluate how equal your relationships are with your customers.

In some industries, one of the biggest barriers to engaging new customers can be the business itself and how it wants to engage with its customers. In many cases, if this is an ongoing relationship, it can often involve a contract for a fixed term, be it for a month, six months, a year, two years, five years or longer in some cases.

From the business's perspective, a contract makes economic and financial sense as it allows them to plan resources in order to deliver against that contract in a profitable way, secures future revenues but also protects them if anything goes wrong.

However, a fixed-term deal that is enshrined in a legally-binding contract can, for some customers, seem like a big commitment and can be the thing that makes the difference between engaging with the business or not. Like it or not contracts scare some businesses and consumers.

Some firms understand this and are innovating around how they engage with their customers and the terms and nature of the relationships they have with them.

INSIGHT IN ACTION

Consumer Cellular is one such firm. They are a rising star in the US mobile (cell)phone industry. In an industry that is dominated by contracts and Pay As You Go (PAYG) options, what they have done is abandon any form of customer contract and then allow their customers to scale up or down their payment and usage plans, at any point, without any long-term commitment or incurring any penalties.

However, the innovative thing is not what they have done but why they do it.

In an interview,[17] Consumer Cellular co-founder and CEO John Marick said that whilst they know that their profitability is all about how long their customers stay with them, they also believe that they can earn their loyalty by always delivering value and great service to them. This, in their opinion, doesn't require a contract.

John also added that, from their customers' perspective, the removal of a contract 'equalises' the relationship between them and Consumer Cellular. This has a huge impact on how their customers feel and behave but it also has a huge impact on the firm's behaviour.

There is no slack, the sort of slack that often comes with a contract. There is no time to take it easy. Every moment, every decision and every customer interaction counts.

This doesn't mean that they can't and don't make mistakes but it does mean that they have to stay focused on service and the value that they deliver, as they don't have a contract to fall back on.

For them, it is the value and the service that they deliver and the emotional 'credit' or track record that they build up with their customers that determines their loyalty, not a contract.

The finance, legal and risk department may not like this type of approach but customers do. According to the 2013 Consumer Reports survey,[18] Consumer Cellular's customers gave them the top customer satisfaction ranking of any wireless provider in the US that year and they have retained that ranking for four years running.

HOW TO USE IT

Contracts are familiar things in business and play an important part in many customer–business relationships.

However, they can also have a negative impact on a customer relationship and can create the impression that when the customer has signed the contract the firm no longer needs to try to engage and serve them to the highest level as they are now locked into a contract.

Consumer Cellular's example shows that some firms are willing to innovate around the conditions of their relationships with their customers and how it has benefited them.

Contracts are often the default option in many businesses and so to assess how you can innovate around the relationships you have with your customers ask yourself these questions:

- How 'equal' is your relationship with your customer?
- Do you use contracts as a default in your business?
- How do your customers feel about that?
- Would you be willing to follow Consumer Cellular's example and give up contracts with your customers?
- If yes, when and how are you going to start?
- If not, why not?
- What else can you do to make the relationships you have with your customers feel more equal?

INSIGHT 18   # DATA, PRIVACY AND THE IMPACT ON CUSTOMER RELATIONSHIPS

Use this to understand the danger around making assumptions about the data preferences of your customers and how best to manage them.

More and more customers are concerned about the amount of data that is being collected about them via their web activity, their apps, their smartphones and so on. In fact, according to a 2015 study[19] by YouGov:

72% of consumers in the UK are concerned about their private information online.

This is backed up by additional research[20] by the UK Information Commissioner's Office (ICO) which shows that:

85% of people are concerned about how their personal information is passed or sold to other organisations.

In addition:

77% of people are concerned about organisations not keeping their personal details secure.

But, different people have different concerns and to differing degrees. To help with this the Direct Marketing Association (DMA) reports a model[21] that suggests consumers can be categorised according to their attitudes toward privacy.

THE CATEGORIES THEY DESCRIBE IN THEIR MODEL ARE:

Privacy pragmatists: These are customers that understand firms will want to collect data on them and they will assess on a case by case basis whether they get value out of the exchange via access to a service or enhancement of an existing service.

Privacy fundamentalists: These are customers who do not want firms to collect personal data on them at all even if it could help enhance or tailor a service to them.

Privacy unconcerned: These are customers who are not concerned about the personal data that is collected about them or what it is used for.

These are useful categories but they possibly ignore some nuances or additional categories that firms need to be aware of. As such, the categories could look something like this:

Customer category	Description
Open	These customers trust companies with their data. They are completely happy with new advances in technology, data gathering, tracking, data sharing and all the personalisation and service enhancement that that can bring.
Selective	These customers are a little more discerning. They are happy to share their data like the 'Open' group but only with some very select and trusted brands and not with others.
Sometimes	These customers are happy to share their data but only want to share it when it suits them. When it doesn't, they'd rather remain like the 'Closed' group below and don't want to be tracked or have any data gathered on them until they are happy to do so.
Closed	These customers don't like the idea of data being gathered on them as they do not know how much data is being collected, when it is being collected, what for and who is it going to be shared with. They like doing their own research, have their own trusted sources that they rely on and are deeply suspicious of the idea of 'personalisation'.
Unaware	This group of customers could be the silent majority who are, possibly, aware of the issues but unaware of what data is being collected on them, how it might be affecting them and what their options are.

If firms don't recognise this emerging set of preferences or categories and make assumptions or take decisions that go against these preferences then things could backfire badly and cause significant damage to their brand and customer relations.

For example, look at the customer backlash[22] that Spotify faced in August 2015 when changes to its privacy policy gave it significantly more access to personal data on its customers' mobile phones. The greater access included permission to access and collect email addresses, details of birthdays, location data and pictures. Spotify's new privacy policy also said that some of the data that would be collected would be shared with advertisers but they did not stipulate what data would be shared and with whom.

This resulted in a huge backlash from customers, particularly on social media, with many users, including some very prominent customers, cancelling their accounts and subscriptions.

In the face of this, Spotify's CEO responded very quickly and posted an apology, an explanation and what they were going to do about it in a blog post on the company's website.[23]

This will not be the last time that this happens and firms need to be careful of customers' feelings and preferences about their data, the data collection methods, what firms plan to do with the data and privacy.

In the face of these issues and in response to customers' concerns, new solutions and approaches are starting to emerge. Customer Managed Relationships (CMR) systems are one such solution that aims to put customers in control of their own data and help them manage the data that they share with the brands that they want to have relationships with.

INSIGHT IN ACTION

Geraldine McBride, CEO of MyWave, is a pioneer in the CMR space and is developing a next generation CMR solution that puts customers in charge of their data and their experience.

In an interview,[24] she described the advantages that CMR applications can bring:

- CMR applications can act like a personal assistant in your pocket and will help connect customers to the brands they want, enabling them to get personalised products and services that treat them like the individual they are as opposed to one of the masses.

- For businesses, these applications will help close the engagement gap between the customer and the business as it allows customers to signal their preferences and intentions, allows for personalisation and enables new and more profitable business models and better experiences for customers.

- If companies shared the data they had on their customers, gave it to them and asked them to update it in their own personal cloud that would allow brands to have real and personalised conversations with their customers about what they really want and what they care about.

- Assuming that customers opt in to this type of arrangement, this would have two clear benefits for brands:

  - better and closer customer relationships with customers; and
  - a lower cost to serve because they do not have to maintain all that customer data.

A report[25] by Ctrl Shift in 2014 estimated that as much as £16 billion in the UK could be freed up through the use of applications like MyWave.

HOW TO USE IT

The data and privacy debate is going to be a growing and developing issue in the next few years.

CMRs and similar types of systems are likely to play a growing role in this space. However, if firms are to protect the relationships they have with their customers they need to start a conversation early to better understand their customers and their concerns about data, privacy and their preferences. Doing so will minimise the risk that they will make assumptions or decisions that run the risk of being wrong, ending up doing more harm than good to their brand and the relationships they have with their customers.

To better understand the data and privacy issues and their customers' preferences, firms in the first instance should:

- work out the data and privacy preferences of their customers and what categories they fall into;
- communicate and agree this with their customers; and
- plan their activities accordingly.

INSIGHT 19 # DESIGN A GREAT CUSTOMER EXPERIENCE BY INCLUDING YOUR CUSTOMERS

Use this to help understand how you can leverage the insight, power and creativity of your customers to help you develop a great customer experience.

Back in 1998, Steve Jobs in a *Business Week* article[26] said that:

> *It's really hard to design products by focus groups. A lot of times, people don't know what they want until you show it to them.*

That's fine for some companies but these days many companies are eschewing Jobs' advice and sourcing great new ideas by getting their customers involved in an innovation process or as an integral part of their business model.

Moreover, what these companies are finding is that asking their customers for their input is a great way to build engagement with their community.

INSIGHT IN ACTION

EXAMPLES OF FIRMS THAT HAVE MADE THIS WORK

In May 2014, McDonalds[27] launched its My Burger® campaign, where it asked members of the public to design and name their ultimate burger. The winners of the competition would have their burgers appear in their 1,200 UK restaurants for a month. The campaign had over 98,000 entries.

Hewlett-Packard (HP) asked[28] one of its most valuable customers, DreamWorks – the innovative film company – how they could improve the HP computers that DreamWorks used to create their animated films. The animators at DreamWorks told HP that they didn't like the fact that the USB ports were on the back of the machine as it made it hard to plug other devices into the workstation. HP listened and moved the USB ports. HP found DreamWorks feedback so useful that they convened a customer advisory group and invited DreamWorks and other firms, some of whom were HP customers and some who weren't, to join it.

Launched in 2008, 'My Starbucks Idea' website[29] is where Starbucks encourages customers to submit ideas for better products, how they can improve the customer experience and how they can improve their community involvement. Since then, they have received more than 200,000 ideas from customers that are then voted on by their community. These ideas have led to the launch of around 300 new innovations by Starbucks.

Threadless,[30] an online commerce business founded in 2000 and best known for selling T-shirts, takes the concept of getting their customers involved to a whole new level. What they do is invite artists and designers from around the world to submit designs to them. The Threadless community then scores each of these designs and the best ones are printed and sold. However, the winning designers profit too and are rewarded with royalties and Threadless gift vouchers.[31]

HOW TO USE IT

Getting your customers involved in the process of designing and developing your customer experience is a great way to build engagement with them as well as adding an extra great source of insight and creativity into the process.

TO START DOING THIS YOURSELF IN YOUR BUSINESS, ASK YOURSELF

Could you benefit from creating a customer advisory group like HP?

Could you create a competition for your customers around innovative ideas for new products and services or how you could improve your customer experience?

Could you ask your customers to design products for you and would you be willing to share the profits from new ideas with the originators?

Want more ideas about how you could include your customers in helping you design your customer experience then check out my interview[32] with Mark Hurst about his book: *Customers Included: How to Transform Products, Companies, and the World – With a Single Step.*[33]

INSIGHT 20 # PEOPLE WILL PAY MORE FOR BETTER SERVICE

Use this to dispel any fears around the idea that customers won't pay for better service or an enhanced customer experience.

Businesses often complain that they are continually getting beaten on price by their competitors. However, when challenged that they shouldn't be competing solely on price, they often go on to complain that their customers won't pay more for better service.

That's simply not true.

HERE'S SOME RESEARCH THAT PROVES OTHERWISE

Oracle in 2012 found[34] that 81% of consumers that they spoke to would be willing to pay more for better service or for a better customer experience. In fact, nearly half of them would be willing to pay more than 5% above normal prices.

American Express in the same year found[35] that around two-thirds of consumers would be willing to spend more (up to 13% more, on average) with a business that they believed provided great customer service.

In 2010, RightNow Technologies found[36] that 84% of consumers that they surveyed said they would be willing to pay extra to get a superior customer experience. The largest majority (88%) would be willing to pay 5% extra whilst 62% would be willing to pay 10% over normal prices. However, the really interesting statistic is that 11% of customers said that they would be willing to pay 25% or more for a better customer experience.

INSIGHT IN ACTION

Businesses often protest when this argument is made but our own behaviour and experience tells us that customers are willing to pay for better service:

- Why do we pay more for first class rail tickets? The train doesn't get there any quicker.
- Why do we pay for priority boarding on flights? All it allows us to really do is get on quicker, sit for longer and the plane, like the train, is not going to get there any quicker.
- When ordering from an online retailer we will often pay more for speedier delivery.

The list could go on and on.

The following example comes from one firm that knows customers are willing to pay for better service and is willing to really put its money where its mouth is. The firm in question is Linley & Simpson, a Yorkshire based estate agency, which launched a new service[37] in August 2015 that allows customers who would like to sell their house to choose how much they pay in fees depending on the quality of the service that they have received. They launched the service after conducting some research and then listening to their customers. Now, whilst customers can still pick a fixed-fee arrangement, their new service is based on a sliding commission scale ranging from 1.5% where customers rate the service they have received as being 'excellent' all the way down to 0.5% where their clients have said that they are 'not as satisfied'.

HOW TO USE IT

Research shows that customers will pay for a better service or enhanced customer experience. However, charging customers higher prices is often met with internal resistance. A lot of which is driven by fear. Fear that customers will leave if they are charged more for a better service or an enhanced customer experience.

One way to combat this, and to test it out on your customers, is to develop a 'premium' style offer that delivers enhanced service for a higher price and sits alongside your normal offer.

You never know, the addition of a 'premium' style offer may just attract and engage a new set of customers.

SECTION 3

SERVE

INTRODUCTION

You've worked hard to attract your customers, you've engaged them and now you need to focus on serving them so that their service experience is easy, simple and memorable thus helping you build a platform for long-term loyalty, advocacy and growth. However, serving customers is one of the hardest parts of business, given its breadth and complexity. When things go wrong it is often heavily laden with emotions. This section, therefore, will aim to cover a range of important issues regarding customer service in the modern world. It will cover topics such as how to make queueing and waiting easier, how focusing on the smaller things can make the biggest difference, what we can learn from behavioural science to help us improve how we serve our customers, why customer complaints are an opportunity, the most important emotions involved in customer service and the benefits of proactive customer service.

EVERY CUSTOMER HATES WAITING BUT THE EXPERIENCE CAN BE IMPROVED

Use this if your customers sometimes have to wait and you would like to make the experience better.

Waiting, or queuing in some instances, is something that no customer really wants to do and is often a source of annoyance and frustration.

In large part, this is down to the fact that when we want to do something, buy something, eat something, ask something or have a problem solved we want to do it now and, therefore, don't like to wait.

The act of waiting, however, is often exacerbated by the fact that most people tend to overestimate how long they have been waiting. Some sources[1] show that we overestimate our wait times by as much as 36%. Meanwhile, another research study[2] by Videlica and Contact Babel found that callers into contact centres who had to wait in a phone queue believed that they waited for an average of 8 minutes, which was 24 times longer than their average wait time of 20 seconds!

However, despite this, many companies don't spend a lot of time thinking about the impact waiting or queuing has on customer service or customer experience. The reason could be that many of them design their waiting or queuing systems with their own processes in mind; this is why queuing is an oft overlooked element and source of frustration in the customer experience process.

Nevertheless, waiting is sometimes unavoidable. David Maister in *The Psychology of Waiting Lines*[3] has an interesting take on this when he says:

> *What matters most in a waiting line is how people feel about the experience rather than the waiting itself.*

INSIGHT IN ACTION

A great example comes from Bill's, a chain of restaurants that started in Lewes, East Sussex, and which has now grown into a UK chain. In their popular Brighton branch, particularly at the weekend, they often have queues of people (sometimes out the door) waiting to eat and, as such, they have employed some really innovative techniques to help manage their queues.

TECHNIQUES THEY HAVE USED INCLUDE:

Acknowledging all customers that come through the door as well as explaining the situation and the process.

They queue customers inside the restaurant and not outside.

They give out menus in the queue.

They allow customers to order drinks whilst in the queue.

They continually communicate with customers in the queue giving them estimates of how long they will have to wait and also point out where they will be sitting once the sitting diners are finished.

These tactics work for a number of reasons:

By acknowledging and communicating with customers they make them feel welcome and less anxious about the prospect of a wait.

By giving them menus and the opportunity to order and have drinks while they wait they make them feel that their buying experience has already started.

Finally, by continually updating the customer about the expected wait time and where they are likely to be seated they make the end of the process seem tangible and less uncertain.

As a result, this makes their customer experience extremely 'sticky'. Their queue management techniques are not 100% reliable but they do work most of the time and have an estimated 70–80% success rate in getting people to queue rather than leave.

HOW TO USE IT

Sometimes it's inevitable that a customer has to wait to be served or have their question answered. However, firms miss an opportunity if they don't try to make the waiting process a bit better.

If you have customers waiting in your business and are worried about how many you lose because of that or how it negatively affects your customer experience, answers to these questions might help:

- If customers have to wait, how can you make the waiting experience more 'sticky'?
- How can you occupy a customer's time while they are waiting in a manner that is engaging for them?

- If they are calling on the phone, can you eliminate their wait and give them a call-back option?
- Can you get your customers started on their buying journey whilst they are waiting in the queue?
- Can you give your customers rolling updates on how long they have to wait?

INSIGHT 22　SPEAK MY LANGUAGE

Use this to help simplify your language and improve your service and the engagement of your customers.

Most businesses can settle, through laziness, habit or other reasons into using their own language when trying to explain and generate demand for or understanding of their products and services. Nowhere is this more so than in industries that are somewhat technical in nature, e.g. medicine, web-design, architecture, accountancy, tax, insurance, law, engineering.

PLAIN (Plain Language Association InterNational) provides a great and very relevant example[4] from the insurance industry:

Here's a piece of sample text that a customer received from their insurance company:

We have recently implemented an enhancement to our computer system that will enable us to provide better service to our valued customers. This has resulted in a slight delay in the processing of your renewal. The difference you will notice is in the payment schedule. Your annual policy premium has been divided over 11 (eleven) months, and as a result your monthly payment will have increased due to the reduced number of monthly instalments.

Now, here's the text rewritten in plain language:

We are a little late in sending your renewal documents because we have made a change in our computer system in order to provide better service. Your annual premium will now be divided over 11 months instead of 12 so the monthly payment will increase slightly.

What we can see is that the rewritten text has been written with the customer in mind so that they understand, very clearly, what has happened and what the implications are for them.

Therefore, it is important to remember when communicating with customers that:

- They will not always understand what you do.
- They will base their opinions of quality on many things, including how you communicate with them and the language you use – your product or service being just a small part.

- The non-core areas of your business are very, very important to how your customer perceives you.
- Customers will often judge your expertise in areas they do not understand by your excellence in areas which they do.

Therefore, using your customers' language will go a long way to improving their understanding and their perception of the experience they receive. This, in turn, will have the effect of increasing engagement and trust, ultimately improving your rate of acquisition and retention.

INSIGHT IN ACTION

Here are some examples that show that even though some businesses and professions are trying to improve their use of language they still have a way to go:

EXAMPLES

In June 2015, the UK's Royal Pharmaceutical Society[5] released a study into sunscreen use. They found that consumers have a 'worrying lack of understanding about the degree of sun protection different products provide' and that as many as 92% of all consumers did not know that the SPF rating displayed on sunscreen labelling does not guarantee good all round protection from potential sun damage. The SPF rating refers to protection from UVB rays only and protection from more harmful UVA rays is typically indicated by another and separate 'star' rating.

In 2014, the UK consumer group Fairer Finance announced the results of a new survey[6] which found that when customers wanted to open a bank account their terms and conditions ranged from just over 34,000 words (HSBC) to 11,000 words (Nationwide). Customers in the car insurance sector face a similar issue where the range of terms and conditions went from over 37,000 words (Endsleigh) to just under 7,000 words (LV). Why is it that some companies can effectively produce the same terms and conditions so much more succinctly than their competitors?

In Ireland, in March 2015, Ireland's National Adult Literacy Agency (NALA) launched a health literacy survey[7] which showed that 39% of patients surveyed would prefer doctors, nurses and pharmacists to use less technical and medical jargon and more understandable language. This was up from 33% in research conducted in 2007.

HOW TO USE IT

It's easier to talk about your business in the language of your industry. However, for customers that's not always the easiest way to understand and makes engaging with them harder.

Here are some questions to help you figure out whether or not you are speaking your customers' language and what you can do about it:

- Are you operating in an industry that is technical (even a little bit)?

- Are you speaking in a language that your customer understands? Or, even better, are you talking the customers' language? If you were to show a sample of your communication with your customers to someone outside your business or industry, your grandmother say, would they understand it?

- How do you know if you are doing this consistently? This approach takes time and effort and, so, when in a rush or when things get busy, it's normal for us to slip back into the language of our profession or, if you like, back into bad habits. So, keep an eye on this and regularly monitor if you are communicating in plain language.

- Want to find out what your customers think? Ask your customers if they understand what you say when you describe your business or service?

INSIGHT 23 NATURE ABHORS A VACUUM

Use this to help understand if you have any gaps in your communication with your customer and what impact they may be having.

In physics, there is a postulate called 'horror vacui', which translates as 'Nature abhors a vacuum.'

In common and personal terms, this can be re-stated as: 'In the absence of information, we make stuff up.'

This has a lot to do with how our mind works and when we have no new information our minds make stuff up as a result of our anxieties, fears, stresses and all sorts of other negative emotions.

This has particular relevance when it comes to the delivery of customer service. Businesses often face situations where they have nothing to report to their customers. However, just because they have nothing to report or no new information to share doesn't automatically mean that their client or customer doesn't want to hear from them or that they shouldn't be in touch with them.

We can call these gaps 'vacuums' in your customers' journey, and if left unaddressed they can cause the kind of emotions that we don't want to be conjuring up in the minds of our customers or clients.

INSIGHT IN ACTION

Here's an example of a 'vacuum' in practice:

Peter (name changed) is an old friend of mine and is in his early 40s. It came as a great shock to everyone when a few months ago he suffered a stroke.

After Peter was discovered following his stroke, he was rushed to hospital where he received treatment. A few weeks later everything was looking good and he was making good progress in his recovery. But, then something suspect showed up on a routine scan.

This is where it got uncomfortable for Peter.

Despite repeatedly asking for more information about his situation, what the scan showed and what the next steps were, Peter was told by the nurses that they had no information and we're waiting to hear from the doctor.

So, he waited. And, then he waited.

While he was waiting, there was apparently a lot of consultation going on behind the scenes but he still wasn't given any information as to what progress they were making, what the next steps were, when the doctor would come and see him or what his prognosis was.

In fact, he waited for a few days for something to happen.

Then, a new scan was scheduled, conducted and was followed by another period of waiting. Eventually, the results came.

The whole waiting process left Peter feeling lost, frustrated, uncertain, anxious and very stressed.

In terms of the prognosis, Peter eventually met with his doctor who told him that they had found an inoperable tumour on his brain and he was immediately scheduled for chemo and radiotherapy in order to try and shrink the tumour and prolong his life expectancy.

Peter's story illustrates how waiting for information, particularly at a sensitive or anxious time, can seem like a very long time and can have a huge impact on, in this case, a patient's experience.

In fact, research[8] shows that in 'life-threatening situations, negative emotions can concentrate our attention on the passage of time and so make it seem longer than it really is'. Other research shows that this can be further compounded by our own efforts to take our minds off our emotions.

What is clear is that whilst they were busy analysing Peter's test results, his doctors lost sight of Peter during the process. They lost sight of how he was feeling during the times that he was waiting for news from them and how that had a huge impact on him and his overall experience.

It's true that, at times, waiting is part of a process and it cannot be avoided. However, what we can do is to be aware of how any periods of waiting affect our customers.

HOW TO USE IT

Whilst working hard to find a solution for a patient, client or customer, don't lose sight of how they might be feeling while they wait and what you could do to make their wait a bit easier. Think about their whole and actual experience.

Don't leave people hanging, keep them informed of what is going on and give them a clear idea of what is going to happen next and when it is going to happen. Even providing information about the ongoing process can fill the 'vacuum' and be just as helpful and comforting as the final answer. Finally, keep in mind that sometimes responses like 'there is no new information' or 'we have nothing to report yet' are still valuable to the customer, client or patient.

INSIGHT 24 BAD REVIEWS CAN BE GOOD

Use this to help reduce fears and anxieties that exist around bad reviews and how you can turn them into opportunities.

For consumers, reading and being influenced by reviews is now a fact of life. In fact, this is supported by research[9] which shows that:

- 77% of UK consumers look at customer reviews before making a buying decision.
- 88% of consumers trust online reviews as much as personal recommendations.
- 90% of consumers claim that positive reviews influenced their buying decision making.
- 86% said that they were influenced by negative reviews.

But, many customers don't just look for good reviews, they also look for bad ones too as many are becoming suspicious of companies that only have good reviews. Jan Jensen, the former Chief Marketing Officer of Trustpilot, echoes this and says that he routinely looks for bad reviews when researching a new company.[10] He learns more about a business by how they respond to negative feedback.

However, most businesses fret about bad reviews online and do their utmost to avoid them. But, the reality is that we have to get used to the idea that negative reviews and feedback are likely to come our way from time to time.

So, the important thing is not to ignore the negative reviews and feedback but to be ready to deal with them, respond to them and learn from them. Often, how we respond to complaints and negative feedback can show the side of our business that does not get seen or talked about much.

INSIGHT IN ACTION

Most customers are pragmatic and realise that sometimes things will go wrong.

So, going out of your way to show how you respond when things do go wrong can (assuming that you do it well) have a hugely positive effect on your reputation.

This is backed up by a brand loyalty study conducted in 2012 by ClickFox,[11] where they found that 40% of customers said that they were 'won over' by a company after the company exceeded their expectations when they resolved an issue with their purchase.

Moreover, TripAdvisor[12] in their research found that 87% of travellers had 'an improved opinion of a hotel after reading an appropriate management response to a bad review'.

Enough said.

HOW TO USE IT

No business is ever perfect all of the time. Therefore, there is a possibility that at some point you will receive a bad review.

Moreover, realise that some customers may be watching to see how you respond to bad reviews as well as looking at your good reviews as it's a good way to find out how good your service is when things go wrong.

So, when you receive a bad review don't do as many firms do: panic, ignore it, hope nobody will notice and then try to drown the bad review in more good reviews.

What you should do is respond as swiftly as you can and aim to resolve the problem as quickly and easily as possible. If you do, you just might keep that customer and win more in the process.

INSIGHT 25 REMOVE THE GRIT

Use this to help you identify and remove the small annoyances in your customer experience that distort the picture and always get remembered.

Often, in a bid to improve their customer service or experience, companies and brands find themselves just focusing on how they can add a delight or wow factor to their customer service or experience. In doing so, they tend to overlook the minor glitches or frustrations customers might have when they do business with them; they risk ignoring the very things that customers tend to remember.

It's a bit like walking to your next meeting or appointment and noticing that you have a piece of grit in your shoe. Now, you may be a bit pressed for time and the grit doesn't hurt so much that you have to stop to remove it. However, it's always there and once you arrive at your destination, what do you remember about your journey? The grit in your shoe, right?

That's all to do with how the memory works and the fact that we, generally, remember feelings, particularly annoyances and disappointments, better than anything else.

The great American poet and author, Maya Angelou, sums up this idea very well when she said:[13]

> People will forget what you said. People will forget what you did. But, people will never forget how you made them feel.

INSIGHT IN ACTION

Ruter, the public transport body of Oslo, uses this principle in improving their customer experience and are continually investigating the things that annoy or irritate their customers. In fact, on realising the power of this insight, Ruter's CEO made a public announcement saying that Ruter's strategy from now on was to 'stop irritating you'.

Doing so has earned him and Ruter a large amount of respect and credibility in Norway.

In practice, Ruter have made a series of small changes in how they operate their business including changes like, while buses are waiting for the right time to depart, they now let their customers wait inside the bus rather than outside in the cold.[14]

HOW TO USE IT

From time to time there will be little things in our customer experience that annoy or irritate our customers. These are often overlooked but shouldn't be as they tend to be the things that customers remember.

If firms want to go about locating and removing the 'grit' in their customer experience these questions will help:

1 Ask your customers a question such as: 'Is there anything that we do, however slight, that annoys you or has annoyed you in the past?'

2 Ask your frontline staff: 'What customer issues or problems keep recurring?'

Asking these two questions will give you a great start and all the clues that you need to start removing the 'grit' from your customer experience and, in doing so, will help you dramatically improve it.

INSIGHT 26 THE PRIMACY AND RECENCY EFFECT

Use this to help you understand and focus on the most important times in your relationships with customers.

There is a concept in psychology called the serial position effect[15] (also known as the primacy and recency effect) that was first coined by Hermann Ebbinghaus.[16] Through his research Ebbinghaus found that when people are asked to recall a list of items that are presented to them, they tend to be able to best recall those at the end of the list (the recency effect) and those at the beginning of the list (the primacy effect) better than those in the middle of the list.

If we apply this concept to our relationships we can see it in action. For example, think back to a boyfriend/girlfriend relationship that you had growing up. It's highly likely, following the serial position effect, that you are most likely to remember the beginning of the relationship (butterflies in your stomach in the run up to your first date, the excitement of falling in love, etc.) and the end of the relationship (the break up, the arguments, the heartache, etc.).

The reason for this is that it is at those times that our emotions are at their highest and most intense and that is why we remember the beginning and the end of relationships more readily.

This also applies to the relationships that we have with our customers and can provide an insight to the quality of the relationships that we have with them.

For example, if a relationship with a customer has not started well or there is no excitement then there is a danger that that will be how it will be defined or remembered in the customer's mind and it is very difficult to change that (first impressions and all that). Further, if it has been a while since you were in contact with your customer then this lack of communication or the quality of communication that you have with them could be the thing that sticks in their mind and makes them think you don't care or don't value their business (perceived indifference).

The lesson here is to be mindful of how we start relationships with our customers and how we continue or maintain them. This could also be the difference between the perception of good customer service, loyalty and retention and the opposite.

INSIGHT IN ACTION

In 2013, Iceland, a UK grocery retailer, showed[17] how to put this insight into action. What they did was implement a scheme where they started to print off 'individually tailored vouchers' for their customers at the point of sale, the till or checkout if you like, rather than sending those vouchers by post.

This was part of a wider customer engagement strategy that they launched in 2012 but by 2013 it had already allowed them to:

- drive new sales and grow their market share;
- dramatically improve customer satisfaction from 65% to 85%;
- collect more data and understand their customers better;
- increase membership of their Bonus Card scheme to an all-time high;
- reduce promotions spend by 16%; and
- increase the amount they planned to give away on promotional vouchers in 2015 to £5 million.

Iceland's new scheme, which leverages the primacy and recency effect, delivers rewards to customers at the end of their shopping experience and this heightens their possible emotions at the end of their 'shop'. This, in turn, increases the likelihood of the retailer being remembered positively, which also increases the likelihood of customer satisfaction at the point of sale and gains customers' ongoing loyalty.

HOW TO USE IT

We know that first impressions count but we often forget that the last impression that we leave with someone can be just as important. The primacy and recency effect captures this and helps firms to understand their power and influence.

Firms wanting to put this insight into action should start by asking themselves a series of questions:

- Are we thinking about the relationships that we have with our customers?
- Do we think the primacy or recency effect is having an impact on our customer service and relationships?
- What sort of first impression are we making with our customers? Could it be better?
- What impression did we leave the customer with at our last point of contact? Was it good? Could it be better?

Answers to these questions will help you think about how you can apply the primacy and recency effect when designing your customer experience and how you deliver great service.

INSIGHT 27 LOTS OF SMALL CHANGES ADD UP

Use this when you need to drive performance improvement and want a more effective way to achieve it.

Some of the best insights into how businesses can increase performance and deliver better service don't come from other businesses. Many of the best insights come from different areas like sport, music, the arts, etc.

One such insight comes from the world of cycling, specifically from the world of the Team GB track cycling and the Team Sky Procycling. The approach taken by Sir Dave Brailsford, the former Performance Director of Team GB and now Team Principal at Team Sky, is based on his philosophy of:

An aggregation of a series of marginal gains.

Explaining in an interview[18] prior to the Beijing Olympics in 2008, Dave Brailsford said:

We've got this saying, 'performance by the aggregation of marginal gains'. It means taking the one per cent from everything you do; finding a one per cent margin for improvement in everything you do.

Brailsford's basic premise is this: a 10% improvement in performance in any given area over a given time period is often hard, daunting and mostly unsuccessful.

However, rather than trying to improve one area by 10%, how about identifying ten different areas where you can make a 1% improvement. This can seem much more achievable and motivating.

The reason that this works is that it's easier to take small steps rather than large steps, and doing so generally achieves a higher likelihood of success. This also helps with generating momentum, establishing sustainable change and overall performance improvement.

Brailsford's and Team GB track cycling and the Sky Procycling teams' achievements over the last few years are a testament to the depth of talent that they have in their team but also to their relentless focus on improving performance by finding those 'marginal gains' year on year.

INSIGHT IN ACTION

A few years ago my wife and I visited Marrakech for a few days and we stayed at Riad Dar Mimouna, a fantastic riad in the old city.

On arriving on the Thursday night, we were shown to our room and one of the first things that we noticed was that there were twin beds in the room and not a double bed.

We didn't make a big deal of it as it was late and we were tired so we quickly pushed the beds together and went to sleep. However, what happened next was the thing that stood out for us.

The next day after being out during the day, we returned to find that our bed had been made into a double without us even asking. It just happened. It was this and countless other things that made our visit memorable and unforgettable.

For me, I think that when we talk about great customer service or creating a memorable customer experience it is easy to fall into the trap that delivering this is about the process that we design and how we train our people to deliver that. However, what was apparent from our visit to Riad Dar Mimouna is that the experience was completely enhanced by the combination of little things that were just done without us asking.

You can only accomplish this type of service or experience through the selection, training and support of engaged employees and an abundance of care.

Great customer service is often about listening and then doing the things that you are not asked to do. The 'one per cents'.

HOW TO USE IT

A large step change in performance in one area is often hard. However, a series of small changes across a range of areas is much more achievable as shown by Dave Brailsford's approach and the successes Team GB and Sky have had in track and road cycling.

To emulate their approach, businesses should take up the following challenge:

- Can you come up with your own list of 'Brailsfords' . . . areas where you believe that you can easily make a 1% improvement in the delivery of service to your customers or their overall customer experience?

Taking up this challenge will help you create an action list and lay the foundation for a customer experience improvement roadmap.

Moreover, taking this type of approach has an additional benefit in that it democratises the identification of areas of improvement, i.e. you can get everyone involved to identify the one per cents. This helps build ownership of any improvement and change initiatives, which, in turn, increases the likelihood that any improvement will be realised.

INSIGHT 28 MAKE IT SIMPLE

Use this to help you rail against complexity in your business and create a culture that is always looking for opportunities to simplify things for you and your customers.

The following are two quotes about simplicity.

Charles Mingus, the legendary jazz bassist, said:[19]

Making the simple complicated is commonplace; making the complicated simple, awesomely simple, that's creativity.

Blaise Pascal, the French mathematician, physicist and philosopher, said:[20]

I would have written a shorter letter, but I did not have the time.

These quotes, hundreds of years apart, explain the elegance, meaning and power in simplicity. Both men also realised that the quest for simplicity was where real magic exists.

Since 2009, Siegel + Gale, the international branding agency, has been tracking the impact of 'simplicity' when it comes to brands. What they have found is that in an increasingly complex world, simplicity stands out when it comes to service and experience. They have also discovered that brands that focus on delivering simple service and experience deliver better results:[21]

- Brands that have a focus on making their experiences simpler have, since 2009, beaten the average global stock index by 70%.
- 70% of consumers are more likely to recommend a simpler experience.
- 38% of consumers are willing to pay more for a simpler experience.

Simpler service or experience pays.

INSIGHT IN ACTION

Here are some examples of firms that are challenging incumbent players and redefining what it means to deliver a simple experience:

CHALLENGING EXAMPLES

Metro Bank in the UK is challenging incumbents in the UK banking sector by recognising what customers find hard about normal banking practice and then delivering a service that addresses the issues. For example:

They recognise that normal banking hours are not convenient for many customers so they open from 8am in the morning to 8pm at night on weekdays and then for most of the day on weekends, allowing customers the chance to visit the bank when it is convenient for them.

They know that opening an account and then waiting for new bank cards can be frustrating for bank customers so they allow them to come into the bank and, providing they have the right information and documents, immediately open an account and walk out again with their own ATM card. The same applies to lost bank cards: customers can come into the bank and they will be issued with a new one straight away.

They know that 25% of all households in the UK own dogs and that owners don't like tying their dogs up outside. Therefore, they welcome dogs into their branches and even provide them with dog-treats and bowls of water.

Fetch Eyewear and **Glasses.com** are taking the risk and guesswork out of buying glasses online. Fetch allows you to select six different frames which they will then send to you so that you can try them on for seven days, returning the ones you don't want – and the postage is paid too. Meanwhile, **Glasses.com** allows you to choose a pair of frames with free prescription lenses and they will send them to you to try on and use for 15 days. If you don't like them, just send them back.

Ovo Energy in the UK has introduced a new service for pre-pay customers that takes away the hassle of running to the shop to top up their prepay gas and electricity meter. Utilising a smart meter, their prepay customers can now top up their meters using an app, online or by text message.

HOW TO USE IT

Making things simple takes time, effort and requires making choices. This can be hard and requires not only physical and mental effort but emotional effort too as we have to choose to give things up or remove them. But it's also a continuous road and the quest for simplicity is an ongoing and never-ending process.

To make sure that you are always looking for ways to simplify your business ask yourself the question below on a regular basis. It will tell you how much attention you are paying to simplifying your business and how regularly you are taking action:

- What have you done lately that simplifies the service or experience that you deliver to your customers?

Moreover, to help you embark on your quest for simplicity also ask yourself these questions on a regular basis:

- What is good about what we do?
- What is not so good?

- What is hard for our customers?
- What is easy for our customers?
- What should we stop doing?
- What should we do less of?
- What should we continue to do?
- What should we do more of?
- What should we do differently?

INSIGHT 29 # BEHAVIOURAL SCIENCE AND LESSONS FOR CUSTOMER SERVICE

Use this to understand when and how to apply some of the latest advances in behavioural science thinking to help improve your customer experience.

Advances in behavioural science in the last ten years have cast a lot of light on how and why people make decisions and behave in certain ways.

This is generating increasing amounts of attention in the business world but, since 2010, it has been a UK government team, the Behavioural Insights Team (BIT), that has been leading the way in the application of behavioural science. This team started life inside 10 Downing Street but, since February 2014, has been incorporated as a private company, jointly owned by the UK Government, Nesta and its employees.

Whilst their work has focused primarily on the arena of public services, institutions and policy, they have consistently released updates on their work and their findings to the wider world to help advance the use and application of behavioural insights. One such update came in 2010 where BIT published MINDSPACE, a mnemonic of what they believe are the nine most robust and non-coercive influences on our behaviour:

MINDSPACE element	Description
Messenger	We are heavily influenced by who communicates information
Incentives	Our responses to incentives are shaped by predictable mental shortcuts such as strongly avoiding losses
Norms	We are strongly influenced by what others do
Defaults	We 'go with the flow' of pre-set options
Salience	Our attention is drawn to what is novel and seems relevant to us
Priming	Our acts are often influenced by sub-conscious cues
Affect	Our emotional associations can powerfully shape our actions

MINDSPACE element	Description
Commitments	We seek to be consistent with our public promises, and reciprocate acts
Ego	We act in ways that make us feel better about ourselves

Source: © Crown Copyright 2012

Applying this to the business world, we can see that the elements in MINDSPACE can have a huge impact on the decision making process. It also shows us that when considering a product or service, customers will tend to be influenced by other things outside the set of benefits normally associated with a product or service.

Therefore, businesses should keep these influences in mind when designing their product, service or overall customer experience. After all, as Nicolae Naumof, an applied behavioural science specialist, suggests in an interview:[22]

We must realise that we are not talking to 'Mister Spock' when talking to or dealing with customers.

INSIGHT IN ACTION

Following the publication of MINDSPACE in 2010, the BIT team went on to develop and publish their EAST framework[23] to help with applying behavioural insights. They found that if you want to encourage a behaviour and/or uptake of a product or service, then you should consider making it easy, attractive, social and timely:

EAST framework elements	Description	Element in action
Easy	Leverage the power of defaults, reduce the effort required and make any messages simple.	Automatically enrolling employees into workplace pension schemes and allowing them to opt out rather than requiring them to opt in was an effective way of increasing pension savings. It was also popular with employees as it made the whole process easy. In fact, in large firms where the scheme was first started, in the first six months participation rates rose from 61% to 83%.

EAST framework elements	Description	Element in action
Attractive	We are naturally attracted to things that are designed well, include images and colours, but also novel incentives.	DVLA found that when letters to individuals who had failed to tax their vehicles included a picture of the non-taxed vehicle in the letter to owner, payment rates rose from 40% to 49%.
Social	Show potential customers how others in a similar situation have behaved, encourage them to spread ideas and actions across their own network and ask them to make a commitment to help others.	HMRC increased tax payments on time by telling people in letters that most people pay their tax on time. Their most successful letter increased on-time payments by 5%.
Timely	As the saying goes 'timing is everything' so think about when customers are most likely to be receptive to any request or proposal. In addition, we are more influenced by costs and benefits that have a near-term or immediate impact. But, there is a difference between what customers say and what they actually do, so help them to identify the hurdles to action and to make a plan to overcome them.	The Courts Service increased the payment of fines by sending those with fines to pay a text message ten days before bailiffs are due to arrive. This helped double the value of fines collected.

Source: © Behavioural Insights Ltd 2014. Not to be reproduced, copied, distributed or published without the permission of Behavioural Insights Ltd.

HOW TO USE IT

Advances in behavioural science have produced some fantastic new insights, many of which can be used to help us improve our service and customer experience. However, when thinking about applying behavioural insights to your business, there are two things that you first have to do:

1   Accept that you are dealing with human beings that are subject to a range of influences.

2 Accept that there is no perfect solution or one size fits all and that you may need to experiment before you find the best solution that fits your business and customer base.

Once you have done that, here are a few questions and ideas to help you start applying behavioural science insights to your business:

■ First, consider your product, service or overall customer experience and give yourself a rating on a scale of 1–10, where 10 is exceptional and 1 is poor, against each element of the EAST framework?

■ Where could you do better?

■ Brainstorm some ideas about how you could better leverage the EAST framework.

■ Put together an action plan to test out these ideas.

INSIGHT 30

IDENTIFY AND DEAL WITH SILENT COMPLAINTS

Use this to understand that silent complaints exist, what to do about them and how to go about identifying and addressing them.

Many companies sit back and revel in their high customer satisfaction scores and dismiss today's complaint as unimportant in the grander scheme of things.

However, customers don't always tell you when they are not happy. In fact, research undertaken by US firm TARP Worldwide (now known as CX Act)[24] back in 1999 illustrated the issue of 'silent complaints'. Their research showed that for every 26 unhappy customers, only 1 (roughly about 4%) will make a formal complaint. The remaining 25, the 'silent complainers', tend to tell all of their friends and family about their experience and, more often than not, decide never to do business with that company or brand again.

But why don't customers complain? Further insight is provided by Call Centre IQ who in an article called 'The Psychology of Customer Complaints'[25] suggest that the three top barriers to customers complaining are:

1 The time and amount of effort that the customer estimates it will take for their complaint to be resolved.

2 How responsive they believe the business will be to their complaint.

3 The customer's own personality type, character and preferences.

Understanding the issues and finding and addressing 'silent' complaints can be a sure road to better service not only in helping businesses retain their customers for longer but also figuring out how to improve their ability to deliver great service.

INSIGHT IN ACTION

Many companies get this and are addressing it via their Customer Success Management (CSM) strategies and teams. One firm that is having great success with this type of strategy is Big Ass Fans, where in an interview[26] their CEO, Carey Smith, told me that the setting up of their customer advocate team, whose sole responsibility is to identify and fix what their customers don't like, has been a core part of what has helped grow their company results fivefold from $34 million in revenue in 2009 to $175 million in 2014.

THE BIG ASS FAN APPROACH

The team is led by Dave Waltz and Carey and Dave went on to tell me that what they are looking for is not a 'pat on the back' but glitches or flaws in the process or product so that they can fix them and then feed that information back into the company so that they can learn and improve.

To do this, Dave asks a set of very simple questions:

Did you receive the product?

Do you have any questions?

Is everything ok?

Their primary objective in every customer transaction is that the customer is satisfied, over and above the profitability of the transaction. Their approach is about finding and fixing any and all of the problems that their customers may have. This has led them to do many things differently from how they design their packaging, to their blister packs for the nuts and bolts that come with the fans, to their pictorial instructions for the set up and operation of their fans.

Much of their insight and the improvements they have made came from conversations that Dave has had with customers. Many companies don't have the courage to do this as they are scared about what they might find out.

Too many companies rely on surveys for feedback, send them out and hope they get something back. However, although Big Ass Fans also send out surveys they don't rely on them, instead focusing more on proactively speaking to their customers.

HOW TO USE IT

Not everyone that has a complaint or isn't happy complains. Moreover, it can take bravery and commitment to ask customers for their honest opinion as sometimes the feedback is critical.

If you think you may have 'silent' complainers in your business, here are a few things you could do to address the situation:

- Average response rates for customer surveys tend to be in the region of 5–15%. So, ask yourself these questions:
  - Are you getting a higher response rate from any customer survey or feedback process that you have in place?
  - If not, for all of those that are not replying, how many could be 'silent' complainers?

- Could this be the reason that you are not getting very many complaints but are still losing customers?
- Could their assumptions about your responsiveness or complaints process be getting in the way of them talking to you?
- Are they maybe too shy to talk to you?

■ In addition, get out and talk to your customers. This might be more straightforward for businesses that have a physical presence as they will have opportunities to see and talk to customers face to face. However, online-only businesses can do this too by selecting a number of customers, particularly the ones that have either only done business with you once or have done business with you a number of times in the past but are no longer a customer, and inviting them to have a chat on the phone or to participate in an email exchange. Once you are in contact with them, listen to their concerns – and don't assume that a customer satisfaction survey is a substitute for this.

INSIGHT 31 CONSISTENCY IN QUALITY AND DELIVERY IS KEY

Use this to help reduce the variability in your customer service delivery due to different skill and knowledge levels across your teams.

In 2013, Consumerist.com, a source of consumer news and information and a subsidiary of Consumer Reports, published an article, 'To Resolve Some Customer Service Problems, Just Call Back'.[27] In the article, they suggest that customers that have not had success with their first attempt at resolving a complaint should 'try calling or e-mailing back to get someone else'.

This implies that if you want good service then you should be persistent and go looking for it. Now, this may be a reliable strategy, as a customer, and not unreasonable. I must admit I've also found myself calling customer services again and again as I've struggled to navigate a particularly cumbersome telephone menu system or to get the answer that I was looking for.

But, is it right that customers have to do this? Isn't there a bigger problem at play here if your customers have to try more than once to get the service they want?

INSIGHT IN ACTION

My wife faced a similar problem, a little while ago, when she found herself locked out of her bank account. She had done nothing wrong but had to call the bank's call centre a number of times to try and get it fixed.

HERE'S WHAT HAPPENED

When she noticed the problem, she called the call centre and spoke to someone, went through all of the security protocols and was assured that the problem was fixed. She then waited for a little while for the system to refresh and then tried to access her account.

The problem persisted.

She called back, spoke to a different person, went through the same security procedure, received an apology for any inconvenience and then the agent claimed to have 'fixed' the problem.

Again, after waiting for systems to refresh, etc. she tried to access her account.

The problem persisted.

By this time my wife was getting very frustrated and quite irate.

She then called back again and spoke to another person. This time, the agent had a look around her account settings and their systems and swiftly located the 'problem'. The agent again apologised for any inconvenience and then stated that they had now fixed the problem.

Again, after waiting for systems to refresh, etc. my wife tried to access her account.

Success! And, a sigh of relief.

Thinking about my wife's experience raised a number of questions:

- Is this good customer service?
- What's the effect on customer experience when something like this happens?
- How is it that some customer service agents can fix things in an instant and others need to be called back again and again to get things fixed?
- Are they having a bad day?
- Are they taking exception to the way they are talked to both by customers and their peers/bosses?
- Is their training or skill-set sub-par?

It's frustrating that customers have to resort to this sort of behaviour. But, putting that aside, I wonder how a chief marketing officer or a chief customer officer or a customer service director feels about the fact that a proportion of their customers have to try repeatedly in order to get what they want.

HOW TO USE IT

Assuming that there were no technology glitches, what's obvious from my wife's experience is that the skill and knowledge levels amongst the agents are not the same. Experience also tells me that this sort of situation is not uncommon.

A way to solve this is to identify the 'super users' amongst your customer service agents and get them to share their top tricks and tips for dealing with difficult or particular issues.

The challenge, however, that organisations face is that many of their 'super users' covet and hoard insight to maintain position and importance. This can be a very human thing (and failing). Knowledge is power and all that. And, they probably believe that knowledge keeps them safe.

But, getting that knowledge out in the open and shared amongst colleagues is one of the greatest challenges businesses face when trying to improve their customer service delivery and the overall customer experience.

So, how do you make 'super users' share? Here are a few ideas that are proven to work:

- Identify your 'super users'.
- Acknowledge them – we all like a bit of recognition from time to time.
- Give them an additional title – call them a guru, if that works.
- Ask them to share their experience.
- Ask them to be a focal point for queries and help in their specialist area by other parts of the team.
- Ask them to mentor and train others.
- Continue to give them recognition and consider giving them incentives and bonuses to help them along their way.

This may cost a little more, in the round, in terms of time, effort, salaries, bonuses, etc. But committing to this and making it work will pay dividends in your First Call Resolution (FCR), Average Handling Time (AHT) and Net Promoter Score (NPS) numbers.

A NAME NOT A NUMBER

> **Use this** to help you understand everything from how you design your systems and processes to how you refer to your customer. It all has an impact on the customer experience.

Many businesses talk about putting the customer at the heart of everything they do and how the customer is their number one priority.

However, many of these companies, when you listen to them talk about their business, talk about the number of accounts or policies, etc. and very few of them will actually talk about their customers directly.

This illustrates not only how many companies organise themselves but that they are organised in a way that is for their benefit and ease rather than those of their customers'.

This flies in the face of trying to be or claiming to be more customer-centric and providing good customer service.

INSIGHT IN ACTION

Here's a story about an experience I recently had with my water company:

- My water company wrote to me about a problem with my account and address details.
- I read their letter.
- It seemed like a clerical error and easy to sort out so I called them.
- I then quoted the **reference number** in their letter to them.
- They couldn't find it on their system.
- I then quoted my **full name, full address with postcode** and my **date of birth** to them.
- They still couldn't find me or any reference to the letter on their system.
- They then asked me for my customer number as they explained that this was my unique identifier!
- I didn't have my customer number to hand (it's not something that I carry around with me) and it wasn't on the letter so we couldn't progress until I gave it to them.

> ■ Now, I didn't have time to start digging into my household files and so what it meant was that I had to log onto my internet banking site and retrieve some information from the **direct debit** that I had set up to pay the water company every month.
>
> ■ I did that and then we got it all sorted. Finally.

This may sound like it is a bit of a gripe and I understand why it is easier to look up an alphanumeric code in a database. But, as a customer . . . I don't care.

Their reference number on their letter should have been enough to initiate a conversation. And, failing that my full name, address, postcode and date of birth should have been enough to get things started.

But, having to do more work to retrieve additional information to help them sort their problem left me feeling somewhat aggrieved.

That, as a customer, shouldn't happen.

HOW TO USE IT

Organising your information and customer data in a way that makes your customer do the work every time they call you may make sense to you and how you structure yourself, but it is not going to help your customer service promise or cause.

Stress test your customer experience by seeing how you respond to a customer who contacts you without their account number or policy number or membership number to hand:

■ Can you locate their information quickly enough?

■ Do you have an alternative route that they can go down?

■ Can you establish and maintain data security?

■ If not, then you should consider re-configuring your systems.

Great service starts by treating a customer as a person and not a number.

MAKE YOUR SERVICE PROACTIVE

Use this when your service is purely reactive and you want to transform it and your customer experience into something more valuable and more proactive.

Whilst proactive customer service is not a new concept, it surprises me that the majority of companies are still only organised to deliver customer service reactively.

Why is that?

Research suggests that one of the primary reasons is that most businesses are organised, run and measured in a way that works against the sort of collaboration and cross-functional working that a proactive customer service strategy would require.

Reactive customer service is both expensive and un-engaging and firms would do well to look at what that type of approach is actually costing them in terms of extra resources and costs versus a more proactive approach, which offers cost saving and customer engagement opportunities.

Here are a few reasons why firms should consider adding a proactive element to their customer service strategy:

1 **There is a clear opportunity to reduce costs.** Research by Sabio and the Customer Contact Association[28] found that between 25% and 40% of all calls to UK contact centres are either unnecessary or avoidable. According to the research, the most common causes of these calls included: customers chasing information about deliveries or updates on what was due to happen next in the purchase cycle; customers calling to clarify issues regarding pricing or terms and conditions; and customers having to call the contact centre again as the contact centre had failed to address their problem first time around. This research is supported by work conducted by the Corporate Executive Board[29] who found that 57% of all inbound calls to a contact centre could largely be attributed to a customer not being able to find what they were looking for on a company's website.

2 **Customers want to be contacted proactively.** A survey by inContact[30] found that 87% of customers surveyed said they wanted to be contacted proactively by a company, when it came to customer service issues. Also, nearly three-quarters (73%) of those who had been contacted proactively and had a positive experience said that

it led to a positive change in their perception of the business that contacted them.

3 **A proactive customer service strategy delivers cost savings and boosts retention.** Further research by Enkata[31] put all of this together and showed that an effective proactive customer service strategy can:

 - reduce inbound customer service call volumes by 20–30% over a 12-month period;
 - lower call centre operating costs by as much as 25%; and
 - has a positive effect on customer retention, boosting it by 3–5%.

These data points clearly outline the opportunity that is in front of many companies.

In addition, in an interview[32] Matt Lautz, President and CIO of CorvisaCloud, a provider of call centre software, went further and said that he believed that proactive customer service would 'pay back in terms of relationship building ten-fold'.

INSIGHT IN ACTION

Analysis of leading companies shows that they realise that relying just on reactive customer service is no longer sufficient in order to compete, differentiate and drive their businesses forward. Increasingly they are now implementing proactive customer service strategies, which is allowing them to lower costs, drive additional revenue, improve satisfaction and NPS scores, increase customer engagement and boost customer loyalty and retention.

Identifying where opportunities to be proactive lie, Kate Leggett of Forrester in a blog post on trends in customer service in 2015[33] suggested that:

In 2015, we expect organizations to explore proactive engagement . . . delivered at the right time in a customer's pre-purchase journey to help answer customer questions.

We are starting to see signs of that but I don't think Kate and Forrester go far enough and there are opportunities to deliver value to the business and the customer not just in the pre-purchase phase of the customer journey but across the whole customer lifecycle (pre-purchase, purchase and post-purchase).

Here are some examples from firms that are leading the way and implementing their own proactive strategies at different stages of the customer lifecycle.

EXAMPLES

PRE-PURCHASE: PROACTIVE SERVICE CAN BEGIN BEFORE A PROSPECT IS A CUSTOMER

US truck rental firm, Budget Truck Rental,[34] has added an intelligent virtual agent from Intelliresponse to its web self-service tool to provide instant answers to questions from prospective customers. Following implementation, they have been able to reduce inbound call centre calls by 28% and achieve $875,000 of cost savings and online revenue gains in the first 7 months of operation.

Similarly, using the same technology and approach, Copa Airlines[35] has reduced its call and chat volume by 40%, which has freed up their live agents' time to focus on helping customers that have urgent and more complex enquiries.

PURCHASE: PROACTIVE SERVICE IMPROVES THE CUSTOMER EXPERIENCE OF EXISTING CUSTOMERS

AT&T is using SmartVideo technology[36] from SundaySky to minimise 'bill shock' for their new and returning customers. 'Bill shock' occurs when the customer is shocked when they receive their first bill and they do not understand all its different elements. This results in a significant number of inbound calls. Now, each new and returning customer receives, along with their bill, a link to a personalised video that explains all of the different elements of their specific bill. Implementing this strategy has allowed AT&T to significantly reduce its inbound calls as a result of 'bill shock', drive an increase in valuable services, like paperless billing, and increase their NPS scores.

Debenhams,[37] a UK retailer, is taking a different approach and uses comprehensive buying guides on its website to dramatically reduce the rate of returns and exchanges that they receive, which saves them costs, frees up resources and improves overall customer satisfaction.

POST-PURCHASE: PROACTIVE SERVICE MAINTAINS AND IMPROVES THE ONGOING RELATIONSHIP

Virgin Media in the UK has around 2,500 engineers providing free-of-charge servicing for their broadband customers. However, through the operation of their business, they know that on average 10% of all their service appointments fail, largely because their customers forget about the appointments. This has huge utilisation and cost implications for Virgin Media. Therefore, in the run-up to appointments they have started to proactively communicate with their customers across various channels, using technology from Contact Engine,[38] to make sure that customers don't forget about the appointment. This is driving a dramatic reduction in the 10% of failed appointments, saving Virgin Media millions of pounds a year in utilisation and engineer costs and, at the same time, is driving increased customer satisfaction and higher NPS scores.

Anglian Water, one of the UK's largest water companies, is also using technology to proactively notify their customers, this time from Aspect,[39] regarding water outages relevant to their location. This has allowed them to save hundreds of thousands of pounds in call centre costs every year and has improved their overall customer experience, which is supported by the positive feedback they receive.

HOW TO USE IT

So, whilst it is true that proactive customer service is not a new strategy, given the clear business case and examples of success that many companies are having it pains me that more companies do not pursue it as a viable strategy given the cost, customer engagement and satisfaction benefits.

However, looking more closely, the main barrier to its implementation seems to be that this type of strategy requires cross-functional collaboration and cooperation.

To overcome these barriers and push forward with the development and implementation of this type of strategy, leaders should:

1 **Investigate:** Use data tools to identify the most frequently occurring customer questions and problems across the customer lifecycle as well as the area with the biggest number of problems.

2 **Design:** Work collaboratively, leveraging technology, to develop effective solutions to identified problems. Given that customer problems exist across the different stages of the customer lifecycle, this will require a collaborative approach across organisational functions to ensure the design and delivery of a successful strategy.

3 **Plan and pilot:** Aim for quick wins to generate momentum and organisational support. Most organisations are still reactive when it comes to the delivery of their customer service. Therefore, in introducing a new proactive approach it is essential that any strategy focuses initially on piloting one or two new solutions to commonly occurring and costly customer issues. These pilots allow the business to test hypotheses, learn, quickly deliver benefits and help build

support for future initiatives. In the UK banking sector, first direct is a leading proponent of this approach and has used a 'Lab' initiative[40] as a vehicle to test new service ideas and concepts.

4 **Measure and adjust:** Pilots will allow the business to learn and adjust for maximum return. Starting the implementation of a proactive customer service strategy with pilot projects will ensure that organisations minimise risk and resource requirements and take a learning and agile approach, thus enabling them to learn and adjust new initiatives so that they deliver the maximum returns. The Brazilian telecoms company, Vivo, benefited from taking a pilot-based approach[41] when launching a new mobile bill payment service and, through its pilot, gained valuable insights into obstacles to adoption and scaling their new service.

5 **Scale:** Once proven, pilots should be released, adapted and implemented across the organisation. Taking an agile and collaborative approach to the development and implementation of a proactive customer service strategy will allow the organisation to minimise risk and start on the road to achieving the significant benefits associated with proactive customer service.

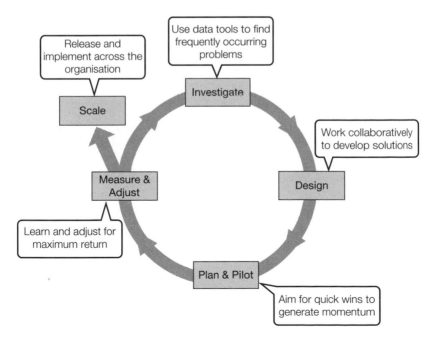

The aim of these five steps is to build trust and engagement both internally (across functions and departments) and externally (with customers) so that both the organisation and the customer benefit.

I hope that more companies take up the challenge and look forward to seeing future examples of valuable and innovative proactive customer service.

INSIGHT 34   MAKE PROMISES, KEEP THEM BUT YOU DON'T HAVE TO BEAT THEM

Use this to understand why it is of paramount importance that you keep your promises but also that there is little payoff in exceeding expectations.

There is a common theory when it comes to customer relations and service that brands should aim to exceed expectations.

That's fair enough, you might say.

But, is there a payoff to exceeding expectations and beating your own promises?

In a 2014 article[42] in the journal *Social Psychological and Personality Science,* Ayelet Gneezy and Nicholas Epley reported that:

> *Breaking one's promise is costly, but exceeding it does not appear worth the effort.*

Moreover, in a pure business context, Involve, the employee engagement agency, conducted a piece of research[43] in 2012 where they found that failing to deliver on promises would result in 68% of all customers cancelling a subscription to a service, and that many of them would not be likely to return.

INSIGHT IN ACTION

A couple of summers ago, on a Thursday evening around 9pm I received a call from my bank.

It was an automated call and, after going through some security checks, the automated voice asked me to confirm whether a series of recent transactions on my bank account were mine or not.

I listened to the details of a series of transactions and indicated that I didn't recognise any of them.

Once I had done that, I was connected to one of the bank's agents, a member of their anti-fraud team. The agent explained that the bank, as part of its anti-fraud efforts, tracks and monitors transactions on my account against my historical spending records and flags up potential issues when purchases are not 'on trend'.

Discussing the transactions with the agent, I told her that I wasn't responsible for any of them and had no knowledge of them. She then said that my bank card had obviously been compromised and that she was going to cancel it, order me a new one, arrange to block any pending transactions on my account and refund me for any that had gone through.

At the end of the call, the agent then told me that my card had now been cancelled and an order for a new card had been placed. She went on to explain that a new one would take up to four working days to arrive.

The wait didn't worry me given that the bank had removed the threat of fraud on my account. But, given that it was Thursday evening and my new card may not arrive until Wednesday of the following week, I was thankful that I had enough cash and other cards in my wallet that would see me through until then.

On Saturday, however, I noticed that my new card had arrived in the post and was ready to use.

I was surprised and grateful to the bank for getting it to me so soon, especially since the agent had mentioned that it could take up to four working days to arrive.

Then, as someone who specialises in customer service and experience strategy, I began to wonder about the whole process.

I began to wonder if the bank and the agent had over-performed? Or, did they just manage my expectations and give themselves the right amount of leeway to make sure that they were able to deliver on their promise?

I don't know.

However, what they did do is not let me down and they kept their promise.

Too often I have experienced and heard stories about firms saying they are going to do something only for them not to deliver or to meet their own promises. This is dangerous.

When it comes to customer service, understanding and serving our customers, companies could do very well by making promises and then making sure they keep them.

HOW TO USE IT

It's common in business to hear someone say that you should aim to exceed expectations. However, the research does not support this assertion. What it does find, however, is that you should always keep your promises and meet expectation but that there is also little payoff in exceeding expectations.

THE IMPLICATIONS FOR BUSINESS ARE SIMPLE:

Don't spend too much time on thinking about how you can exceed expectations.

Spend more time on making sure that you deliver on any promises you make.

To find out how you are doing on those consider doing the following:

- List out the sorts of promises that you are making in your business on a regular basis whether that's keeping appointments, delivering on time, calling someone when you said you would, etc.
- Evaluate how you are doing against these promises.
- If you are not at 100% on meeting basic promises then you'll have identified some great areas for improvement that will pay service, experience and retention dividends.

IMPROVE YOUR SERVICE BY MAKING IT EASY FOR CUSTOMERS TO HELP EACH OTHER

Use this when you want to build a customer support community to help improve your service.

Many firms face rising competition and pressure on prices and costs. Yet, at the same time there is an increasing appetite for better service and customer experience.

This can often be an expensive mix.

To combat this, many firms are implementing customer self-service solutions that help them provide the support that their customers want in a low-cost way. In fact, Forrester's research[44] shows that this is also going down well with customers as up to 72% of them report that they prefer self-service to service over the phone or via email.

One of the most effective, but also one of the hardest, methods of self-service to get right is customer help communities.

The reason that they work is that most customers' problems aren't new so having access to other customers that have faced similar problems in the past can prove very useful. Moreover, as pointed out elsewhere in this book, customers tend to trust each other more than they do organisations.

However, customer communities don't just happen. You can't just build a customer help and support community and expect things to just happen.

Communities are built. And, when done right they can help firms save costs, build engagement and advocacy, and improve service, by getting out the way of customers and allowing them to help each other.

INSIGHT IN ACTION

Zimbra, a producer of community and collaboration software, has been helping Texas Instruments since 2008 to create both external customer help communities (Texas Instruments have roughly 90,000 customers from around the globe using their customer community platform) and internal collaboration communities.

In an interview,[45] Rob Howard, the Chief Technology Officer of Zimbra, explained that customer communities can deliver a range of benefits to firms. One of Zimbra's clients used their community to reduce call deflection, another (a hardware manufacturer) saw purchase rates by customers using communities increase by 24% whilst yet another used community feedback to change their manufacturing process so as to minimise problems that many of their customers were facing.

Rob goes on to suggest the following top tips for making your customer community work.

TOP TIPS

Create lots of unique content within a community that will help to draw your customer in.

Allow your customers to engage with it, comment on it, share it freely and add to it.

'Technical' people are often seen as not being great content creators. Rob disagrees with this and believes that 'technical' people are great content creators and are happy to share their knowledge.

In fact, Rob finds that often 'technical' people are better at creating content and also better at operating in customer facing forums than customer support people. The reason is that they are more invested in the product, solving the customer's problems and the work that needs to be done.

To make a community work:
- First, define the community's business objective, i.e. customer support, customer service, internal collaboration, etc.
- Second, don't start a whole business initiative. Start with one business line, in one region, experiment there and get it right before rolling it out.
- Third, empower your community managers and your great customers. Gamification can help with this. Zimbra have found that there is always a small group of customers that are hungry and ready to help. You just need to find them, enable them and then recognise their participation.

To get communities started and to kick-start internal participation it can be really helpful to 'appoint' people as champions or to publicly recognise them as experts. This adds kudos to their role and promotes participation.

In Rob's experience, communities work best when the product or service that is on offer has some level of complexity to it.

> However, if you have a simple product or service then a customer community works best when it is focused on the use or application of that product and service.

> The most valuable part of creating a community is the data that it creates and the insight it offers.

HOW TO USE IT

Customer help communities, when done right, can deliver significant value and take a firm's self-service strategy to a new level.

So, if you are thinking about building your own customer help community to support the delivery of your customer service, here's a checklist from Rob that outlines 9 characteristics[46] of 'world class communities':

1 Have a clear idea of why you want to build a customer community and what you want it to achieve.

2 People like dealing with real people so make it personal (use profiles with photos, avatars and bios) and don't make the language too technical if it doesn't need to be.

3 Make customers feel welcome and that they belong.

4 Make it easy for people to find the answers that they need.

5 Listen and learn from your community and they'll help you understand how you can improve your products, services and, even, the way that you do business.

6 Highlight and engage your biggest fans and they will help you grow your community.

7 Understand that a little recognition for your community participants will go a long way.

8 Have a clear set of guidelines and make sure people know how they will be enforced.

9 Communities will have members and non-members. Make sure that you make your members feel special and give them members' privileges.

THE LONGEST LASTING EMOTIONS IN CUSTOMER EXPERIENCE

Use this to understand the most dangerous and damaging emotions when it comes to customer experience and what to do about them.

I'm really interested in the emotional and psychological side of customer service and customer experience. As a result, I'm always on the lookout for new and interesting research findings that can inform and provide insight into customer experience strategy decisions.

One piece of research that I came across, via PsyBlog,[47] was published in the journal, *Motivation and Emotion,*[48] in February 2015 by Philippe Verduyn and Saskia Lavrijsen of the University of Leuven in Belgium. Their study focused on finding out which emotions last the longest and why.

What they found was that 'sadness' is the emotion that tends to last the longest as it tends to be associated with major events in our lives, particularly those that have a long-lasting impact such as bereavement. What they also found was that whilst sadness may be the longest lasting emotion, 'rumination' (i.e. time spent thinking about why 'this' happened) is a key and central factor in why some emotions last longer than others.

What's interesting from a customer service or customer experience perspective is that the service or experience that we deliver creates emotions within our customers. But, the research shows that more negative emotions, like disappointment and anxiety, seem to last the longest. Therefore, we would do well to take this into account when designing and delivering our customer service.

INSIGHT IN ACTION

To make sense of these research findings in customer service and customer experience terms, let's assume that the emotions associated with delighting customers include:

- surprise,
- being touched,
- gratitude, etc.

And the emotions associated with service failure include:

- disappointment,
- anger,

- irritation,
- anxiety,
- stress, etc.

Comparing these two groups and the length that each emotion lasts suggests that the emotions that we would normally associate with service failure or customer service problems will last around 3.5 times longer than emotions that we would associate with delighting our customers.

Because these negative emotions last longer, they are, therefore, likely to have a bigger impact and be more likely to be remembered than those associated with delighting customers.

HOW TO USE IT

Emotions play a huge part in customer experience and research shows that the emotions associated with service failure linger the longest in customers' minds.

Therefore, leaders should ask themselves the following questions:

- Is your customer experience and customer service perfect all of the time and every time?
- If your answer is 'Yes', then you have nothing to worry about.
- If your answer is 'No', then your top priority should be focusing on efforts to minimise situations that could create disappointment, anger, irritation, anxiety, stress or other associated emotions.

This might not be as sexy as focusing on delighting your customers but it is likely to have a bigger impact on your customers' overall experience, how you are remembered and what your customers think about you.

MAKE SURE DELIVERY IS NOT YOUR ACHILLES' HEEL

Use this to identify and solve potential problems with the delivery part of your customer experience and make sure that your last leg is not your weakest link.

Often a customer's experience with a delivery or service person at their home/office may be the only face-to-face experience that they have with your company. Therefore, that experience could determine the whole trajectory of their relationship with your business.

When it comes to retail deliveries, Angela O'Connell of MetaPack reckons[49] that 'customers are 59% less likely to order from a retailer again if they have a bad delivery experience'.

However, 'delivery' problems are not just related to retail deliveries. They expand to all industries that utilise 'service' appointments. According to Dr Mark Smith of ContactEngine,[50] '10% of all service appointments from broadband installation to the delivery of a bag of sand to a doctor's appointment fail'.

Delivery problems or failed service appointments can have huge cost implications for firms as well as a negative impact on the customer experience. However, it's often not an area that gets as much attention as it deserves thus making it the Achilles' heel of many firms.

INSIGHT IN ACTION

Here are two stories about two 'delivery' issues and two different approaches.

First, a story about bed buying and delivery. This story involves my mother-in-law, let's call her Mary, who needed to buy a new bed and have it delivered. Having bought and paid for the bed, she arranged for it to be delivered on a certain date within a certain time window. She also made arrangements to take time off work and waited patiently on that day for the delivery to arrive. This is where things started to go wrong. First, the bed company called and moved the delivery time from the agreed morning slot to a slot in the afternoon. Then, they called again saying that they would need to reschedule the delivery date as one of the delivery men had realised that the bed was missing a part and that they couldn't fully assemble it without the part. This was when Mary started to get angry and she called the customer service desk only to be treated as if she had been the one that was at fault. She was also told that she may face additional charges. Faced with no other option she threatened to refuse delivery of the bed. Only then did the customer service representative decide that the bed should be delivered that day after all and that one of the delivery guys was to hot foot it over to the depot, which was only 3–4 miles away, to pick up the missing part and return to Mary's house so they could finalise the bed's assembly.

My second story involves a book that I bought as an advance purchase on the internet. As it came into stock, I received a message that it had been dispatched and that it would take 4–5 days to arrive. When a week passed and it hadn't showed up, I contacted the bookseller and told them of the situation. The first thing they said to me was 'Don't worry. We take full responsibility for this.' Nice. I felt at ease. Then they explained that there had been a few problems with the postal service lately and asked if I could wait for another few days to see if it showed up. I agreed and waited. The book still didn't show up after the agreed time so I contacted them again and explained the situation. They said, 'Don't worry. We take full responsibility for this,' and then gave me three options:

- a full refund;
- a credit on my account with them to the amount I had spent; or
- a replacement book and they would pay the post and packaging.

I chose the last option as I wanted the book anyway. It arrived a couple of days later.

This level of service made me tell a large number of my friends about how I had been treated and how they should use this bookseller.

I think the difference in the price of each item is irrelevant in these stories as the most important thing is how each company responded when one of their customers had bought an item and had paid for it to be delivered. In each case, the business has lost or won a customer for life based on how they responded to what went wrong.

HOW TO USE IT

As much as you might try, no business is going to be able to achieve a perfect delivery record. As a result, it's important to be prepared for when things do go wrong because if you don't then it could have an inordinately large and negative impact on the overall customer experience.

So, to prepare for when things do go wrong you could:

- Work out different scenarios of what could go wrong with deliveries.
- Based on those scenarios, work out what you can do to respond to those problems and fix them as quickly as possible.
- Put in place processes and procedures to support these responses.
- Train your people on your new approach so they understand what to do when things go wrong.
- Realise that you won't have been able to imagine every possible scenario so empower your employees to also use their initiative, within limits, to solve customer problems as they come up.
- However, when problems do fall outside these limits, give your employees guidance on how to efficiently and effectively address these problems so that they can be resolved quickly.
- Monitor your performance, learn from your mistakes and adjust so that your approach gets better and better over time.
- Finally, if you outsource your delivery, be careful, specific and exacting of the standards and the expectations that you demand from the supplier. In the end, they are the ones that are delivering the final leg of your customer experience.

INSIGHT 38 REDUCE EFFORT

Use this when you need to focus on reducing your customers' effort by making things easy and why it's important.

In 2010, the Customer Contact Council, a division of the Corporate Executive Board, undertook a piece of research where they surveyed more than 75,000 consumer and business customers about their recent customer service experiences across a range of channels. They then published their results in a *Harvard Business Review* article, 'Stop Trying to Delight Your Customers'.[51]

Two headline findings emerged from the research that have implications for customer service and customer experience:

1 Aiming to delight customers does not build customer loyalty. However, reducing the effort that customers have to expend to get their problem solved does build loyalty.

2 Leveraging this insight, i.e. reducing a customer's effort, can help firms deliver improved customer service, reduce service related costs and decrease customer churn.

INSIGHT IN ACTION

Nicola Millard, Customer Experience Futurologist at BT, has been exploring this issue in detail. In an interview,[52] she told me that BT's research shows that, across the UK:

- Customer loyalty is in decline and only 50% of customers say that they are now loyal.

- Customer satisfaction and loyalty are correlated. But, satisfied customers are not necessarily loyal.

- Moreover, additional research done in conjunction with Moira Clark of the Henley Centre for Customer Management[53] at Henley Business School found that:
  - If firms satisfy their customers and they don't notice then there is not a lot of point.
  - Customer satisfaction is often seen as a 'hygiene' factor.
  - But, if satisfaction is important to your customers then make sure you satisfy them. Otherwise, focus on making things easy and keep on looking for ways of making improvements.

- On the back of this research, BT are now developing a concept called 'Customer Easy', which is loosely-based around the Net Promoter Score (NPS)[54] approach.

- The output is a 'Net Easy' score, which works on a three-point scale, where −1 is for difficult, 0 is for neutral and +1 is for easy.

- BT are now using this in the consumer division of their business and through that have found that a positive Net Easy score drives an improvement in their NPS score.

- They also know that people that find it difficult to do business with BT are more likely to churn, whilst those that find them easy to do business with are likely to stick around and remain customers.

- They believe that NPS is a difficult metric for the contact centre to affect but Net Easy is much more effective as it allows them to compare the 'easiness' of channels and it focuses on what is of value to their customers.

- BT have collected data on what channels customers find the easiest and hardest to deal with over the last two years. What they found was that post is their hardest channel to use, for both the customer and BT, and web chat is the easiest channel. Voice, IVR (Interactive Voice Response) and email are all bunched in the middle.

- Finally, their data shows that 'Easy' has a high correlation with customer loyalty, retention and positive NPS scores.

HOW TO USE IT

Customers value and reward service and experience that is easy and doesn't take a lot of effort. Therefore, when thinking about your customer experience and customer journey, for each stage of that journey ask whether your approach supports customer success and low-effort and makes it easy for the customer.

If it doesn't, identify the issues and fix those first.

In addition, focus your effort on the following:

- Fix or make the channels that are most likely to be used by the customer easy.

- Don't be content with resolving the issue at hand, think about problems that other, similar customers have further down the line and fix them too.

- Get in touch with dissatisfied customers or those that have had a hard time and ask them for feedback on how you could make your service easier or reduce their effort.
- Track the number of times that you have had to say 'No' or 'We can't do that' to a customer and address those issues. It is possible that they are pointing to a policy or a procedure that is making the customer's life difficult.

IS CUSTOMER SERVICE GOING TO GET WORSE BEFORE IT GETS BETTER?

Use this to understand that firms are facing increasingly high and rising customer expectations and what can be done about it.

We know that a company's ability to deliver excellent customer service is increasingly becoming a source of competitive advantage.

However, many companies are struggling to keep up with the pace of change as well as rapidly changing and evolving customer behaviour and expectations.

Therefore, despite their efforts some companies are facing a scenario where customer expectations and changes in behaviour are moving so fast that, in the short to medium term, they can't or won't be able to keep up.

This may mean that, in the eyes of their customers, some firms' customer service may appear to get worse before it gets better.

INSIGHT IN ACTION

Here are two UK studies published in 2015 that support this idea and offer different perspectives and challenges on how companies are performing and what their customers think.

THE CUSTOMER'S PERSPECTIVE

In January 2015, the UK's Ombudsman Services, which provide dispute resolution for the communications, energy, property and licensing industries, published a report, *Consumer Action Monitor*,[55] which found that over the previous year there had been a significant increase in the number of customers making formal complaints to businesses and an increasing propensity by customers to complain. In detail, they found that:

66 million complaints about products or services were made in 2014, almost double the number made in 2013.

47% of consumers made a complaint when faced with a problem with a product or service, compared to 34% the previous year.

Customers' increased appetite to complain is underpinned by a growing cynicism about company motives with 33% of consumers reporting that they believe big businesses are only interested in money.

80% of consumers say they are unlikely to put up with poor service without taking action, up from 67% the previous year.

HOW COMPANIES ARE PERFORMING

In March 2015, Eptica released its annual Multichannel Customer Experience Study,[56] which evaluated the customer service capabilities of 100 leading UK companies by measuring how they responded to relevant questions sent to them via their web, email, social media and live/web chat customer service channels. The aim of the study was to replicate the experience a customer would receive and to provide a set of meaningful results across different channels. The highlights from the report were:

The web comes out on top as the best channel for delivering customer service with surveyed companies successfully answering 64% of questions, on average. This was an improvement over 2014 levels but the report then raised some serious concerns about the growing gap between the best and worst performers.

More and more companies are offering customer service via email and, generally speaking, email performance was reported to be improving. However, the report also raised concerns that the level of accuracy in email responses is falling.

Social customer service improved significantly in 2015 in terms of response times and accuracy but, again, concerns were raised that performance is patchy.

Web chat leads the way in terms of accuracy and speed. But, it doesn't seem to be getting the commitment and resources that it needs: 25% of the companies surveyed offered web chat but when the survey was conducted only 9% of companies had it working.

Finally, the report found that despite advances in technology and systems, companies were still struggling to deliver consistent responses and answers across channels. The report concludes that this is leading to confusion in the minds of customers but, at the same time, is also driving higher operational costs.

Combining the results from these two reports suggests that:

■ Customer expectations are rising faster than many firms' ability to deliver.

■ There is a real risk that, in customers' eyes, the perception of customer service for many firms could get worse before it gets better.

HOW TO USE IT

Customers' expectations are rising and their propensity to complain is increasing. Therefore, companies need to either step up their service and experience efforts and improve investment, resourcing and performance across the board or, potentially, face a rising tide of complaints from their increasingly demanding customers.

However, don't be frightened into doing too much too quickly. The best approach is a simple and steady one:

■ Understand the existing situation.

■ Identify areas for improvement.

■ Make a plan.

■ Implement.

■ Measure progress and success.

■ Learn from mistakes.

■ Repeat.

The pursuit of a great and sustainable customer experience is a long game and we can learn much from the old saying: 'More haste, less speed.'

INSIGHT 40 WHAT'S YOUR BRAND'S CUSTOMER SERVICE PERSONA?

Use this when you need to better understand how you deliver customer service, where you are strong and what you need to do to improve.

For a number of years, personas[57] have been used by marketers and user experience designers to help them understand customers more and serve them better. The personas that they create tend to be detailed profiles of fictional customers that might use a website, product or service in a similar or particular way.

Personas are also used in psychometric testing and personality tests and allow people to better understand themselves and those around them.

Experience from these two areas shows that understanding who you are, who you would like to be or who you would like to serve is a crucial starting point in any development and improvement journey.

So, wouldn't it be helpful if we applied personas to how an organisation delivers its customer service?

Organisational 'customer service personas' would help organisations better understand themselves, their style of service, where they are strong and weak and what they need to do to improve or transform their 'persona'. Moreover, they would also provide a strategic narrative to any customer service or customer experience transformation initiative.

INSIGHT IN ACTION

In late 2014, Aspect released a piece of research[58] that surveyed customer service decision makers, based on their investment, approach and attitudes towards delivering customer service. Through their research Aspect were able to identify five different customer service personas for organisations:

Persona	Description
The Traditionalist	These firms are keen to please their existing customers and always put them first. They empower their people to do what it takes to make their customers happy with only 5% of them saying that they put more effort into acquiring new customers than they do into taking care of existing customers. Their focus is on building long-lasting relationships, which often requires a high degree of human touch. As a result, they are often slow adopters of technology and any customers that want to contact them via tweeting, live chat or email are likely to be disappointed.

Persona	Description
The Honcho	These type of firms' commitment to customer service is driven by their leaders who are involved in everything from strategy to implementation and all the way through to measurement. These firms are starting to utilise and leverage technology when it comes to delivering a better customer experience but they are not yet using it in the most effective ways.
The Selfie	These firms use tons and tons of new technology and think they are doing everything right when it comes to customer service. However, their Achilles' heel is that they tend to have an over-inflated view of themselves: 95% of them believe that they are doing a better job than customers would say they are doing.
The Casualist	This persona has good intentions but is far too casual in its approach to customer service, i.e. there is no leadership, no alignment with corporate strategy, no metrics and little use of innovative technology to improve the customer service experience. Whilst they can provide a pleasant customer service experience, it's not always consistent or effectively delivered.
The Stickler	This persona is all policy and procedure and no personality. Employees have strict guidelines about how to deal with customer issues but have little flexibility and discretion when it comes to solving more complex customer problems. Whilst they say that service and retention are important priorities, they're not likely to be seen showing appreciation for their customers or exceeding their expectations.

Can you see your company or brand in one of these personas?

HOW TO USE IT

Using customer service personas can give firms an insight into their customer service style. Picking a persona or a combination of personas that most closely describes your organisation is an exercise in awareness. Experience shows that the best and most productive starting point of any development or improvement journey is honest assessment of who and where you are as an organisation.

Therefore, achieving that awareness will help you identify where you are strong, where you are weaker, where you are lacking in personality or process or where you could benefit from the addition of a useful bit of technology.

However, looking at the personas again it is possible to cobble together an 'ideal' or super persona if we take a number of the individual strengths from the different personas including:

■ the customer obsession of the Traditionalist;

■ the technology enthusiasm of the Selfie;

■ the executive commitment of the Honcho; and

■ the policy tidiness of the Stickler.

Combining these traits would help create a customer service approach and persona that addresses the changes in consumer preferences that we see happening around us whilst also delivering a positive financial return.

So, here's what you should do:

1 Pick a persona that best describes your organisation's approach to customer service. If you are unsure which persona you are then take Aspect's customer service persona test: **www.aspect.com**

2 On the four dimensions of the super persona, rate yourself out of ten on each one? Where are you strong? Where do you need to improve?

3 The outcomes of this exercise will produce a quick development plan of what you need to concentrate on if you are to improve your customer service.

SECTION 4

KEEP

INTRODUCTION

You've done the hard work of winning new customers and now comes the work of keeping them as customers, keeping them satisfied and keeping them loyal. Too many businesses relax once they have won a customer and that is their biggest Achilles' heel and the biggest threat to the sustainability of their businesses. Therefore, this section will share a number of insights, case studies, interviews and tips covering a range of issues surrounding a business's ability to attract, retain its customers and grow its relationship with them, including topics such as understanding the differences that exist in your perceptions of how you think and how your customers think you are doing, how you can improve loyalty by improving how you deal with complaints, why improving loyalty and retention doesn't need to be a costly affair, how you can increase loyalty by getting your customers more involved with the story of your own business, why most loyalty schemes don't create loyalty, why you should never become complacent when it comes to your customers, how you can earn your customers' loyalty, why you can't buy it and what really drives loyalty.

INSIGHT 41 THE HOLE IN THE BUCKET SYNDROME

Use this when you need to build awareness around the importance of a customer retention strategy.

Do you know this song from your childhood?

> *There's a hole in my bucket, dear Liza, dear Liza,*
> *There's a hole in my bucket, dear Liza, a hole.*
> *Then fix it, dear Henry, dear Henry, dear Henry,*
> *Then fix it, dear Henry, dear Henry, fix it.*

The song, 'There's a Hole in My Bucket' is a children's favourite, and one that I am sure many of you have heard of and may even have sung as a child. It tells a story where, ultimately, Henry needs water to wet the stone to cut the straw to plug the hole. Yet, he has a hole in his bucket so cannot collect any water . . . deadlock.

The moral of the song is that if your bucket didn't leak water then it wouldn't need to be repaired in the first place.

Applying this to business and thinking about customer retention, i.e. keeping customers and not losing them to competitors, it's clear that a sustainable growth strategy would focus a significant amount of effort on keeping existing customers as well as acquiring new ones.

However, many companies still focus most of their efforts and resources on acquiring new customers and leave much of the retention of customers to chance. In fact, Econsultancy reported[1] that in 2014, 40% of companies were more focused on customer acquisition than retention, 15% were more focused on customer retention and 45% had an equal focus on acquisition and retention.

Unless you are a start-up where you need to focus all of your attention on acquiring customers, companies that neglect retention can end up facing an uphill battle to meet their growth targets.

For example, a friend of mine used to run a division of one of the UK's largest software firms. On taking on the role, he was given a 10% a year growth rate. But, the division was also churning (losing) customers at a rate of 10% a year. This meant that, in reality, if he didn't do anything about the rate that they were losing customers he would have to grow the business by 20% a year to hit his target.

I like to call this 'The hole in the bucket syndrome'. What's the point of putting all that effort into acquiring new customers if you are losing customers at the same rate. Would it not be better to have a strategy that combines acquiring new customers with one that focuses on 'fixing the leaks' and minimising the number of customers that churn each year?

Doing your best to fix a 'leaking bucket' will save time and money, build your brand and result in a more sustainable business.

INSIGHT IN ACTION

Looking at the statistics, the scale of the 'The hole in the bucket syndrome' becomes quite alarming. For example:

- According to a 2013 Harvard Business School Working Knowledge paper by Aurélie Lemmens and Sunil Gupta,[2] US credit card providers often have customer churn rates of around 20% a year whilst European mobile phone companies can have churn rates in the 20–38% range every year.

- A 2010 Pitney Bowes research report,[3] on preventing 'customer churn', provides a more comprehensive view of the size of the customer churn problem across a number of B2B industries in the US, UK and across Europe. They found that the average churn rate for B2B industries was around 11% a year but this varied widely across different industries.

Here are some examples of the average churn rates for selected B2B industries:

- 24% – Office supplies
- 16% – Insurance companies
- 16% – ISPs
- 13% – Banking services
- 12% – IT support
- 11% – Electricity suppliers
- 6% – Accountants
- 5% – Lawyers

The report goes on to list a number of reasons why customers churn. Here's their list in order of descending importance:

- Slow customer service
- Late delivery of service

- Doesn't ask about customer needs
- Not in touch
- Not told about updates and developments
- Call centre can't answer questions
- Doesn't recognise my value
- Irrelevant marketing
- Only email queries allowed
- No online self-service
- Low marketing, low visibility

Now, imagine the impact on your customer retention if you took some of your resources and focused them on some of these concerns.

HOW TO USE IT

A solid customer retention strategy is the foundation of any growing and sustainable business. Why go to the effort of finding, attracting, acquiring and then serving that customer if you are not going to work hard to keep them.

To identify how much importance you put on retention in your organisation you should:

- First, calculate your customer churn rate, where: Churn = The number of customers lost in a period/The total number of customers at the beginning of the period.
- Second, figure out how much of your marketing budget is focused on retaining customers?

These two numbers will tell you a lot about how much you value existing customers, how much you care about them and how much effort you are willing to expend in keeping them.

If you don't like what you see, then change it.

INSIGHT 42 DIFFERENCES IN PERCEPTION EXIST AND MATTER

Use this to identify and address the blindspots that exist in the delivery of your customer experience.

Back in 1955, two American psychologists, Joseph Luft and Harrington Ingham, devised the Johari Window Model whilst researching group dynamics at the University of California, Los Angeles. It is used as a tool for illustrating the differences that exist in understanding between individuals and/or between groups. In the model (see below), there are four areas:

1   **Public** – what is known by the person/group about themselves is also known by others.

2   **Blindspot** – what is unknown by the person/group about themselves but is known to others.

3   **Private** – what the person/group knows about themselves that is not known to others.

4   **Unknown** – what is unknown by the person/group about themselves and is also unknown by others.

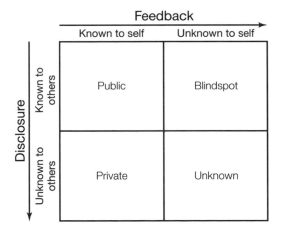

The area that is of particular relevance to business and customer service is the 'Blindspot' area, which highlights the differences that can exist in perceptions between how you think you are doing versus how your customers think you are doing. To illustrate its use in practice: imagine asking an executive in your business for their opinion on how you are doing at customer service and then going and asking your customers for their opinion on the same question. Very often you'll get very different responses.

The difference in opinions can be put down to various things including perception, experience, empathy and views on what is important. These differences, however, can cause real and significant issues when it comes to the delivery of customer service and retaining clients.

The only way to minimise your blindspots is to ask, and keep asking, your customers for feedback on what is important and how you are doing.

INSIGHT IN ACTION

In 2005, Bob Thompson, CEO of CustomerThink Corporation, conducted a piece of research for RightNow Technologies (now part of Oracle) called 'The Loyalty Connection: Secrets To Customer Retention And Increased Profits'.[4] It illustrates this difference in perspectives very well. Part of the research looked at the differences in perceptions that exist between business and customers and what Thompson found was that:

- When customers were asked why they had stopped using a product or service:
  - 74% said that customer service was the major issue;
  - 32% said that it was a quality issue;
  - 25% reported that it was a pricing issue; and
  - 14% said that it was related to functionality.
- However, when business executives were asked for their opinion about why customers had stopped using a product or service:
  - 49% said that price was the major issue;
  - 36% believed that their customers' needs had changed; and
  - only 22% believed that their customer service was at fault.

That's quite a difference in perception.

Jamie Anderson, Global Vice President at SAP, in an interview[5] sums up this situation and challenge very well when he quotes a Robert Burns' poem[6] ('To A Louse'):

O wad some Power the giftie gie us
To see oursels as ithers see us!

HOW TO USE IT

Every business is different, but what is clear is that businesses should stay vigilant about the real reasons why customers leave and should continually, through surveys, conversations and via their employees, be gathering feedback from customers and monitoring how they are doing on an ongoing basis.

Here are some practical steps that businesses can take to help them uncover and eliminate their blindspots:

1 **Recognise and embrace the fact that you may have blind-spots** – increasing awareness of a problem is the first step on any improvement or development journey.

2 **Profitability and decision making** – when decision making is driven primarily by a drive to maximise profitability it will have consequences for customers. Analyse and understand the impact on your customers when decision making is solely driven by profitability. When the business and its employees are solely focused on maximising revenue and profitability, customer experience, service and loyalty can come a distant second and can suffer as a result.

3 **Always be sceptical** – once firms have chosen a particular course of action they can sometimes 'fall in love' with their idea and lose perspective on whether their chosen path is working or not. Look for alternative opinions so that they can challenge confirmation bias,[7] i.e. our natural tendency to look for information that confirms our own view. Always set milestones and goals for projects and strategies to gauge progress and be willing to change tack if the chosen course is not meeting expectations.

4 **Listen to the market** – social media has given us a tremendous ability to research and listen to what the market (customers and competitors) are doing and saying. Tracking what customers are saying about your product or services and what they are saying about your competitors will give you a very useful counter view of your chosen strategy.

MOST LOYALTY SCHEMES DON'T CREATE LOYALTY

Use this when you want to generate more value out of your customer loyalty programme.

When companies think of customer loyalty or loyalty programmes many often jump straight to the sort of incentives that they can offer to their customers to make them stick around.

Sure, people like things for free. Or, more for less. Who doesn't?

But, in many cases that sort of tactic is no different from a price promotion. Moreover, according to a piece of research by fast.MAP[8] in late 2013:

- 96% of consumers would be tempted to switch loyalties to a competitor by a good price promotion.
- 20% of consumers will switch loyalties if offered a better loyalty programme by a competitor brand.
- 33% use loyalty programmes to try out and buy from brands they wouldn't normally use.

This idea is supported by other research[9] by The Logic Group and Ipsos MORI in 2011 who found that:

- 68% of the consumers they surveyed reported that they were members of supermarket loyalty schemes, but that only 47% of them said they were loyal to the supermarket.
- Customer loyalty schemes don't necessarily drive loyalty.
- Customers want something 'special' in exchange for their loyalty.
- 71% said that they would like better offers or services.
- 48% said that they would like better customer service than other customers.
- Customers said that they like 'free stuff' and rewards. But, if presented with a good enough and better offer then they will buy from another business or brand.

Therefore, having an incentive-based 'loyalty programme' is no guarantee that your customers will remain loyal.

INSIGHT IN ACTION

However, that doesn't mean that you should throw out your current loyalty programme if it is only incentive based. Just realise its limitations and don't think that just because you have a loyalty programme in place that customer loyalty is taken care of.

Moreover, if you want to continue with an incentive-based programme then make it more targeted or do something clever or creative with it to make it stand out and resonate with your customers.

A great example of a creative twist on a traditional loyalty scheme comes from Phil Barden, author of the book, *Decoded. The Science Behind Why We Buy,* who in an interview[10] tells a story of one business that was using a traditional customer loyalty card with its customers. However, they implemented a new card scheme where their new loyalty card had more spaces than their regular card but had the first two spaces pre-stamped, i.e. regular cards had eight spaces and the new cards had ten spaces with two pre-stamped. They ran both cards together to gauge the impact of the new cards on sales and loyalty. As it turned out, the pre-stamped card generated 70% more business than the regular card.

However, what's even more fascinating is that the people that went on to complete the pre-stamped cards rated the business as better and had higher satisfaction than the people that went on to complete the unstamped cards.

The reason that this particular tactic works is due to a psychological effect called the Endowed Progress Effect. A 2006 study[11] in the *Journal of Consumer Research* by Joseph Nunes and Xavier Drèze found that:

people provided with artificial advancement toward a goal exhibit greater persistence toward reaching the goal.

HOW TO USE IT

Too many firms don't work hard enough on the design of their loyalty programmes and leave much of their success to chance. However, research by McKinsey[12] shows that the key to building a customer loyalty programme that works is in the detail and the best programmes tend to focus on the groups of customers that:

- can have the greatest impact on any business, i.e. the most valuable ones;
- those with the highest potential; and
- those that are at risk of leaving.

Moreover, McKinsey's research goes on to show that the most successful loyalty programmes have the following characteristics in common:

They have clarity on what their programme is trying to achieve. Doing so will help you target the right sets of customers, design and deliver the most appropriate benefits as well as identifying the best metrics to measure performance.

They dig into the data to find their most valuable customers. Many loyalty programmes use frequency of purchase as a proxy for customer profitability. That is not always the case. Customer data should be analysed to clearly understand which customers have the greatest profitability and sales influence. Your programme should then be tailored to reward these customers and to provide incentives to stay.

They build variegated loyalty programmes. McKinsey talks about 'Published' and 'Unpublished' elements of successful loyalty programmes.

- Published programmes are often those that are publicly available but then tend to be tiered, segmented or tied to different stages of the customer lifecycle. They also tend to be accompanied by different levels of benefits depending on the customer's value or potential. In practice, this can be seen in programmes that have different levels such as bronze, silver, gold and platinum.
- Unpublished programmes tend to be private, invite only and in many cases tend to be more experiential in nature. For example, many brands will invite their best customers to an exclusive product launch, a sporting event or a fancy dinner as a way of making them feel special and part of an exclusive club.

Review your loyalty programme with these characteristics in mind and see how you compare to the best.

INSIGHT 44   MARGINAL COST BUT HIGH PERCEIVED VALUE

Use this to identify the small and cost effective things that you can do to generate a great level of customer loyalty.

When brainstorming ideas and strategies to boost the length and value of their customer relationships, many firms come up with lots of fancy and expensive ideas to try and boost their customer retention and loyalty. However, most of the time all they end up doing is giving their clients expensive gifts, which quite often don't have a significant impact on how long they keep their customers for.

It's easy to buy cheap or expensive gifts but it's much harder to buy and give a meaningful gift – something that shows how well you know your customers and how much you care about them. However, the most meaningful gifts can often be the ones that cost less in money terms but require an investment in time, thought and creativity.

The key to identifying these sorts of 'gifts' is to think about how your business can be more useful and valuable to your customers. The ultimate is to come up with ideas and strategies that have a marginal cost to your business but a high perceived value to your customer.

INSIGHT IN ACTION

Here's an example of a marginal cost but high perceived value initiative that has helped boost one company's customer retention and loyalty:

Established in 1983, Howdle Bespoke Furniture Makers make very high-end bespoke furniture. Their business is almost completely referral based and their customers don't like to be sold or 'marketed' to. As a result, the business has struggled in the past to find a way of staying 'front of mind' with their customers and has often found it difficult to generate both repeat business and new referrals.

Here's an example of one of the things that they have done to build their loyalty and relationships with their clients:

- Many installations, whether kitchens, beds, bookshelves, etc., will 'settle' and 'bed-in' over time meaning that some of their parts will need slight adjustment, tightening or re-aligning at some point.

■ Understanding this, Howdle came up with an idea to offer a free 'service' or health-check for the work they had done for all existing and new clients six months after installation.

Once they had come up with the idea, they started to call their clients. Their first call was well received and delivered their first 'service' appointment.

On arriving at the agreed time, the Howdle team member found that very little adjustment was needed due to the high quality of their installation work. However, the client was delighted with the new service and promptly scheduled £20,000 of new business!

Not bad for a bit of brainstorming and one phone call!

HOW TO USE IT

People often discount the impact that small things, gifts or actions can have on relationships and loyalty. Mother Teresa captured this really well when she said:

It's not how much we give but how much love we put into giving.

Therefore, to better understand what you can do to build increased loyalty with your customers ask yourself the following questions:

■ How well do you know your customers?

■ What can you provide them with that has limited incremental cost to your business but offers high perceived value to your clients?

■ What can you provide them with that shows them that you care, that they are important to you and that you want them to stick around?

INSIGHT 45   MAKE YOUR CUSTOMER THE HERO

Use this to help understand the benefits of putting your customers' stories at the heart of your customer loyalty programme.

When compiling your sales and marketing pieces, who is the 'hero' in those pieces? Do you focus only your product or service? If so, you are in danger of missing an opportunity.

Build better and longer relations with your customers by weaving them into your history and by telling stories where they are the hero, not you or your product or service.

Doing so is a great way to show your customers that you care about them.

A great example of this came back in 2012, around the time of the London Olympics, when Proctor & Gamble (P&G) produced its 'Thank You Mom' commercial.[13]

The theory behind the campaign was that behind every athlete and aspiring champion, there was an amazing mother. As a result, the commercial told stories of a number of mothers and how they support their children on their journey towards their Olympic dreams. In the stories, each mother gives their child the support, strength and courage to not give up on their Olympic dream and they ultimately see them compete in the Olympic Games and achieve their goals. The commercial ends with an end credit screen that reads: 'P&G Proud sponsor of Moms'.

This is classic 'hero' storytelling, where P&G has turned mothers everywhere into the heroes of P&G's story and their products are only there to help them and their children achieve. This campaign helped them build emotional involvement and attachment with their target market, which, in turn, had a substantial impact on customer retention and sales. According to an AdAge article,[14] P&G were looking to generate $500 million in sales on the back of these campaigns and retailers that had launched the campaign with in-store displays reported between 5% and 20% uplift in sales for P&G products in the run up to the London Olympics.

INSIGHT IN ACTION

A smaller but no less effective example comes from an old client of mine, an interior designer, who was struggling to reconnect to her old clients, particularly those that she had not seen and spoken to for more than 18 months.

The client believed that sending them a letter or just calling on them would not be sufficient to engage them.

So, exploring a few ideas she realised that her business would be 25 years old that year. This prompted the idea of assembling a coffee table book celebrating 25 years of her company. However, the difference with this book was that she decided she wanted to tell the story of her company through client stories and photographs of the work that she had done for them and their homes.

To kick off this project, my client started calling round and explaining the concept to her old clients and that she would like to organise a time to come round and photograph them, the work that she had completed for them, their homes, so that it could all be included in the book.

The reaction was very simple: who would refuse the honour of being asked to be included in a book?

The result? My client was able to reconnect with her old clients, reinvigorate her relationships with them and, by making them the hero of her story, drive a large amount of new and repeat business.

HOW TO USE IT

Customers relate to stories that are about them. However, you can't just make your customers the heroes of your story. Here are the steps that you need to take to be able to do that:

- First, you have to get to know them, understand where they come from, what worries them, what they really want, what they currently don't have and then gain their permission to make them the heroes of your story.
- This isn't always easy information to find out but the best place to start is by asking them, listening to them and paying close attention to them.
- Once you have done that, go through all your sales and marketing materials and remove all of the stories that are just about you.
- Then, replace them with stories of how your customers describe your company and products in the context of how they use them and how they have helped them achieve their own objectives.

Making your customers the hero of your story will help you build better relations with your customers, make more sales with existing and new customers, and keep your customers for longer.

WHAT DRIVES LOYALTY?

Use this to understand that customer loyalty is dependent on more than the design and delivery of a loyalty programme.

As we have seen, many loyalty programmes don't drive loyalty and many only attempt to buy loyalty from their customers.

So, what is loyalty? Well, loyalty is about being loyal and supporting something through thick and thin.

Seth Godin, an American best-selling author, entrepreneur and marketer, in a blog post called Loyalty[15] has a slightly different take and suggests that:

> Loyal customers understand that there's almost always something better out there, but they're not so interested in looking.

So, what drives loyalty?

LOYALTY HAS A NUMBER OF ELEMENTS TO IT:

Having a shared cause or interests that are aligned.

Doing what you say you are going to do when you say you are going to do it.

Showing up regularly.

Being able to forgive someone when they make a mistake.

Admitting when you are wrong and then apologising.

Always acting in the best interests of the people whose loyalty you are trying to earn.

We can see from this list that loyalty has large emotional and behavioural elements to it and often is not given – it is earned. Therefore, to earn loyalty, first we have to become the person or the business that people would want to be loyal to.

After all, don't we align ourselves with people and things that are like us, share our values or embody what we want to be like?

INSIGHT IN ACTION

An interview[16] with loyalty expert Steve Sims, Chief Design Officer & Founder of Behavior Lab at Badgeville, offers some clues as to what drives loyalty. Through his research and experience, Steve says that:

- Many, if not most, businesses design their loyalty programmes for their own benefit and fail to take into account what customers want.

- To design a good loyalty programme, businesses really need to understand their customers as people, their motivations, their context and frequency if they are to design a loyalty programme that works better.

- Loyalty is a lot like a habit. This has a lot to do with how we tend to look for patterns and consistency on a conscious and sub-conscious (habit) level and our natural tendency to move towards things that are rewarding to us or away from things that are threatening to us. Therefore, the more positive experiences that a customer has with a business, the more likely that their cumulative experiences will develop into a habit.

- However, even good loyalty programmes suffer from habituation over time as novelty and interest wanes. Therefore, defaulting to traditional, tactical, episodic marketing campaigns to sustain interest over time is unlikely to work and firms need to innovate and think both creatively and strategically if they are to build and sustain their customer's loyalty.

HOW TO USE IT

We know that customer loyalty is about more than a loyalty programme and has large emotional and behavioural elements to it and that loyalty is often not given but it is earned.

Moreover, Steve's insights offer some broad conclusions for businesses thinking about redesigning or revamping their customer loyalty strategies, programmes and initiatives. In summary, here's what firms should do:

- Put your customer, not your business, at the heart of your loyalty strategy and programme.

- Understand your customer as a person, not just as a 'wallet'.

- Realise that your overall customer experience is just as important to your customer loyalty as your loyalty programme is.

- Like any relationship, if your loyalty programme doesn't change over time then your customers are likely to lose interest.

INSIGHT 47 COMPLAINTS ARE KEY TO RETENTION

Use this to understand the important role that complaints play in the customer retention process and how best to deal with them.

Let's play a game of word association. If I said: 'Customer complaints!', what would you say? Any of the following?

■ 'Customers are tricky and they are forever trying to get stuff for free.'

■ 'Some of my customers are idiots.'

■ 'Is there no end to what they will complain about?'

■ 'Why don't they just read my email and the instructions I sent and everything would be okay?'

■ 'They only ever complain about minor stuff.'

■ 'Why can't they say anything positive?'

Let's ask another question. When faced with a customer complaint, how do you react? Do you:

■ tremble with fear;

■ put your 'dukes' up or adopt a 'Crouching Tiger, Hidden Dragon' defensive stance; or

■ do you seek to listen and engage?

The reason I ask these questions is that how we think about customers and customer complaints is key to how we react to them.

In reality, a customer complaint is simply a statement of how someone has been let down and how something or other has not met their expectations. Right?

But, it is also an opportunity for a business to respond, to listen, to show they care and to solve a problem.

Seen like this, when a customer complains to a business it's like giving the business a gift (although sometimes it can look and feel like a gift that is heavily disguised, I admit) but it is up to the business to decide how and if it wants to carefully open this gift to see what's inside.

Complaining customers are still customers, after all. And, customers who take the time to complain often still have some confidence in the business. In many cases, rather than complain it can be easier for the customer to take their business elsewhere, so those who do complain send a clear signal that they want to stay as your customers and are showing a degree of loyalty.

INSIGHT IN ACTION

How you handle customer complaints can have a significant impact on customer retention as a result of a phenomenon called the Service Recovery Paradox. In the entry for the Service Recovery Paradox on Wikipedia[17] it states that:

> a good recovery can turn angry and frustrated customers into loyal customers. In fact it can create even more goodwill than if things had gone smoothly in the first place.

Now, the research[18] on this phenomenon shows somewhat mixed results but it does find that the Service Recovery Paradox is most likely to occur when:

- The cause of a complaint is not considered to be severe.
- The customer has no history of complaining.
- The customer does not think that the company had much control over the cause of the complaint.

HOW TO USE IT

Nothing is ever perfect all of the time and sometimes things will go wrong. As a result, customers will complain but it is how we deal with those complaints that can have a huge impact on whether we keep or lose that customer.

So, when faced with a customer complaint, here's a really simple way (the LEAD method) of handling complaints that I learned from Mark Blackmore of Lammore[19] at a client seminar called 'Delight from Dissatisfaction':

Elements	Description
L – Listening to understand	This step is key when trying to defuse any tension that may come with a complaint. Not listening to someone's complaint is the quick route to having an unhelpful argument. Therefore, listening to someone's concerns is key to defusing the situation and understanding their issue.

Elements	Description
E – Empathise and take responsibility	Empathy (trying to understand their position) is different to sympathy. You need to focus on them and understand their position. Phrases like 'I can understand how that would make you feel' and 'I can see why you feel that way' can be very useful in this context. But, be careful not to collude. Next, you need to accept responsibility for the problem and make it your problem not theirs.
A – Ask/propose a solution	Once you have developed an understanding of the situation and the customer knows that you have taken responsibility for the problem you are now in a position to come up with a proposal to remedy the situation. However, make sure that you share and agree this with your customer.
D – Deliver on the promise	Finally and this is the most important part as it will define the lasting impression that you leave with your customer, always do what you say you are going to do when you say you will do it. Be true to your word. It's personal for them so make it personal for you.

INSIGHT 48 WHERE YOU EARN LOYALTY

Use this to understand where you can earn the loyalty of your customer and what you can do to improve it.

In many businesses, when a customer purchases a product or service, customer loyalty and customer service are often thought of and treated separately. However, research[20] by ClickFox in 2012 found that the most critical times for generating loyalty were at the point of purchase or when a customer had an issue that needed resolving. Going into more detail, their research found that:

- 49% of people surveyed said that their loyalty was earned at the point of purchase/service.
- 40% of the people surveyed said that loyalty was also earned when they had a customer service issue that needed to be dealt with.

Wise companies know that opportunities to generate loyalty exist across the customer experience and, as such, they design and deliver customer experiences that identify and maximise those 'loyalty' moments.

INSIGHT IN ACTION

For example, imagine you have a customer that you have spent some time with and they've just completed a purchase. Now, in the process you've probably got to know them a little better. Or, if they are an existing customer you probably know quite a bit about them already. So, how about once they have completed their purchase you give them something that you know they will like and enjoy just as a way of saying thank you for their purchase?

Here is an example of this sort of thing in practice:

A friend of mine works for a Saudi Arabian residential construction company who focus exclusively on developing affordable housing. When they are working on a development they take daily pictures of the construction site and each house built. Primarily, they do that as a record of the work that they are doing and to document the building process. But, what they have now started doing is to take those pictures and then develop them into individual and personalised hardback books for each new house owner. The book is then handed over to the customer when they are given the keys to their new home. This little extra initiative surprises and delights their customers as it allows them to see the development of their house from the ground up. Through this the business has been able to generate a significant amount of loyalty and positive word of mouth.

HOW TO USE IT

Any time your company comes into contact with customers is a 'loyalty' moment and offers up a number of opportunities where you can add a little extra to the experience and thus improve customer loyalty.

In an interview,[21] Stan Phelps of 9 Inch Marketing describes these little extras as 'Lagniappe' – this is a southern Louisiana and Mississippi (Creole) term meaning a small gift presented by a business to a customer with the customer's purchase *or* an extra or unexpected gift or benefit.

If you are thinking about what sort of little extras you could add into your customer experience, Stan has written a book on the subject called *What's Your Purple Goldfish?*

The book started as a project to crowd-source 1,001 examples of little extras that companies do for their customers. It took Stan over two years to collect all of the examples and the best 100 made it into the book.

However, Stan has made the full list of over 1,000 examples available via the Purple Goldfish Project website (**http://list.ly/list/1Ni-purple-goldfish-project**). Check it out as a source of great ideas for your own set of little extras.

SECTION 5

REFER

INTRODUCTION

So, you've attracted the customers that you want, you've engaged them to the point that they want to buy your products or services, you've provided them with a great experience and flawless service and you've worked hard to keep them as customers for a long time. You've done most of the hard work and if you've done it well enough your customers should be talking about you and referring you to others. But, not wanting to leave anything to chance you now want to make sure and do all you can to turn your customers into an even bigger asset where rather than just being customers they become advocates and active referrers of your business to others. This might happen naturally and does for many businesses. But, leaving it to chance puts a great opportunity at risk.

Leading firms don't leave this to chance as they know that referrals from your customers are the best form of marketing you can do. Therefore, this section will share a number of insights, case studies, interviews and tips covering a range of issues surrounding a business's ability to nurture, encourage and generate referrals from its customers including topics such as why you should always ask your customers for referrals wherever possible, why referrers are not all built the same, how your proactive service can drive referrals, how you can build your own customer referral community and how to get people to talk about you.

INSIGHT 49 IF YOU DON'T ASK THEN YOU WON'T GET

Use this simple tactic when you need to drive an increase in customer referrals.

So, your product or service is wonderful, your customer service and customer experience is good too and your customers are hungry for what you provide. You're getting to know your customers, building trust and insight and keeping your customers for longer. But, your growth is being held back because your customers are not referring you on to new customers and you're stumped as to why not.

Now, words of wisdom can come from unusual places and many of them tend to be statements of commonsense that are not that common. This time the words of wisdom come from my Mum (and probably everyone else's Mum too for that matter). Remember, the saying:

If you don't ask then you won't get.

This is a statement of the obvious but many firms don't ask for referrals from their customers and assume that they will flow naturally if they do a great job. This can happen but it is not guaranteed. The danger being that your business is not always at the front of your customers' minds. So, if you want them to introduce you to, or recommend you to, someone new then sometimes you just have to ask.

INSIGHT IN ACTION

Hinge Research Institute surveyed[1] 500 senior decision makers at industries including management consulting, accounting and finance, marketing, technology, legal services, architecture, engineering and construction about what they considered were their firms' top challenges in 2015. Some 72% responded saying that attracting and developing new business was their top priority. Moreover, the survey went on to find out that 62% were planning on driving this new growth through more referrals.

In a more focused piece of research,[2] InvestmentNews in late 2014 asked a number of financial advisory firms if they had a strategy in place for generating client referrals.

What they found was:

- 70% of a typical financial advisory firm's new business is generated through referrals;
- but, 69% of them did not have a strategy or process in place for asking for referrals from third-party professionals; and
- 66% did not have a strategy or process in place for asking for referrals from their clients.

That means that the majority of these financial advisory firms do not have a formal strategy in place for the element that generates the largest part of their new business.

In my experience, this is not an uncommon situation.

HOW TO USE IT

Are you like the financial advisory firms and don't have a strategy and process in place for asking for and capturing referrals from clients and contacts?

If so, here are a few things that you can do to start generating customer referrals:

1 Start as you mean to go on and give a referral first. Sometimes, you have to give before you can receive.

2 Be gracious, thank and recognise the customers that are introducing you to new people. They may want to be rewarded and that's OK. But, many will refer you on to potential new customers just because they like what you do and doing so makes them look and feel good too.

3 Some customers and contacts will want to be rewarded for referrals so create a referral programme that provides them with some type of reward – benefit in kind, gift or financial – for the business they refer to you.

4 Other people just don't like referrals or don't feel comfortable making referrals. If they don't then ask them if they will help you in other ways. For example, could they be the subject of a case study or could they write you a recommendation or a testimonial?

5 Customers will often 'pigeon-hole' a business as they will only ever buy one or two things from you. Therefore, they may not be aware of everything that your business does. Understand this and help to educate them.

6 Finally, don't forget to ask for referrals.

INSIGHT 50 PROACTIVITY DRIVES ADVOCACY TOO

Use this to understand the link between your customer service strategy and the level of referrals that you receive.

In the 'Serve' section we discussed proactive customer service and highlighted the impact it can have on operational costs, satisfaction and customer retention.

However, there's an additional benefit that comes from implementing an effective proactive customer service strategy, particularly at the post-purchase stage of the customer journey, and that is, if done well, it can really drive brand advocacy and word of mouth recommendations.

Why? Because those little anticipatory extras are unexpected, they can be very useful, they can delight and they can make a customer's life easier and help them avoid any potential problems.

INSIGHT IN ACTION

Here's a personal story of how proactive service can drive advocacy.

A few years ago my brother and his family were living in New York and my Mum and Dad were planning on going to visit them.

When they were planning their trip my brother and his wife recommended that they did not just book a cheap flight but that they book a 'good' flight. They also recommended that they consider flying with Virgin Atlantic as they had flown with them a lot and really like them as an airline. After a little bit of resistance, my Mum and Dad took their advice and booked a couple of economy tickets flying out of London Gatwick.

A few days before they were due to fly, my Mum received a call from someone at Virgin Atlantic, called Kevin, to inform them that they could check in online, to ask if everything was OK, to enquire if all of their passports, ESTA forms, etc. were in order and if they had any dietary requirements for the flight.

This was not a scripted call but was from a Virgin Atlantic customer service representative who was calling to sincerely enquire if everything was OK and if they needed anything. Kevin then asked my Mum if they needed any more leg-room. My Mum thought this was funny and replied that she didn't think so as they were both 5 foot 4 inches tall and that leg room was not an issue!

Now, I do not know if this is a normal part of Virgin Atlantic's customer service offer, if my Mum and Dad were picked for some reason (i.e. they were older and first time travellers with Virgin) or if they were phoned at random. The reasons don't matter to this story. What matters is that Virgin, through its actions, created two new advocates for their business with a short phone call. And, that was for a couple who are not frequent flyers, had not indicated that they had any specific requirements and were not Business or Upper Class passengers.

A few years on from that phone call, my Mum and Dad still talk about it as a stand out and memorable piece of service.

Virgin Atlantic's actions show that a small personal touch can have a huge impact on the overall customer experience and a company's ability to create brand advocates.

HOW TO USE IT

Yes, you can segment your customers, look for common issues and then send a pre-emptive set of emails or text messages at the appropriate time. The financial investment will be relatively low and you'll be able to scale and replicate this with ease.

But, will it have the emotional and advocacy impact that you are looking for?

If you want to drive real advocacy through your proactive service, consider tactics that will have a greater emotional and advocacy impact.

For example, compare these two things:

- a call or visit from a well-trained representative from your company; and
- an email or text message from your company.

If both are delivering the same message, which will be more memorable and which one is likely to have the greater impact?

It may cost you more to phone selected customers and it does take a greater degree of emotional labour, skill and confidence to just call someone out of the blue. However, I'd like to ask you to consider that if you show up for your customers in ways that take effort, thought and creativity they are much more likely to talk about you than if you use other, more common, tactics. It's also these little things that may help you stand out from your peers and, whilst you are helping your customers, you are also making it easier for them to talk about you.

INSIGHT 51   # HOW YOU CAN BUILD YOUR OWN CUSTOMER REFERRAL COMMUNITY

Use this when you want to build a customer community that will help support and drive higher levels of referrals.

We all know how important positive word of mouth and advocacy is to the growth and success of a business.

We've also established that to get customers to refer you to new customers sometimes you just have to ask.

Yet, some companies ask and still struggle to generate referrals. That's not to say that their customer experience isn't great. Their customers tell them that they think they are great and are happy to talk about them. But then, they never do.

This can happen for a number of reasons, including:

- Sometimes customers need a bit of encouragement and structure to help them speak up and share the good things that you do and that you are worth talking about.
- Some customers don't always realise how powerful their advocacy can be.
- Sometimes they just need a bit of a 'carrot' to help them develop a new habit of sharing.
- Often, customers are not always thinking about you and you are not always at the front of their minds.

Faced with this type of situation, leading companies have built their own customer referral communities that aim to help, educate, encourage, support, reward and recognise their customers for their referrals.

INSIGHT IN ACTION

One company that is tackling these issues head-on and is having great success with its own customer advocacy programme is Brainshark. In an interview,[3] Joan Babinski, founder and vice president of marketing at Brainshark, described their customer advocacy programme and how it has benefited their business.

Brainshark launched their Customer Champion Programme in 2012 and to date have been able to recruit more than 400 customer champions. This has resulted in a four-fold increase in the number of companies willing to serve as referees for them, has more than doubled Twitter activity around their brand, has accelerated their sales cycle and has allowed them to build better and deeper relationships with their customers. Further, as recognition of the success of their programme, Brainshark also won a Forrester Groundswell Award in 2013.

Brainshark's success is based on the understanding that there is a difference between what customers say they will do and what they actually do. As a result, their programme is built on two pillars:

1 **Organise and nurture**

   - To give themselves the best chance of success, they decided they had to first organise and nurture their potential advocates if they were to deliver the results that they wanted. To do that they spent a lot of time identifying their potential advocates, understanding what would be of value to them and then building a reward system that was aligned to their profiles and preferences.

   - Through that process they found that the best reward and incentives for advocacy were not always financial. Therefore, their system offers rewards that range from points that can be redeemed against gift vouchers to free training to tickets to a local industry event all the way through to badges and social recognition.

2 **Employee involvement**

   The next essential pillar was the realisation that building a customer advocacy programme is not just a marketing initiative and, to make it successful, it would require the involvement and buy-in of all of their customer-facing employees. Therefore, to complement their Customer Champion Programme, they developed an employee champion programme and have now integrated the two. This has been very effective because:

   - Customer-facing employees are often in the best position to identify potential customer champions and Brainshark's employees can earn their own rewards for identifying good candidates to invite onto the customer programme.

- Whilst Brainshark often challenges their customers to provide testimonials for them, their experience shows that customers often forget or don't follow through on it because they are not always sure what is required of them. Moreover, through experience they have learned that customers are more likely to provide a testimonial if their account manager asks them directly and talks them through the process. Again, Brainshark provides incentives for their employees to ask their customers for testimonials and provides rewards if they find a customer willing to participate.

Many companies fail to generate customer advocacy despite delivering great customer experience and service whilst others are just frustrated at the ineffectiveness of their own customer advocacy efforts. Regardless of which camp you are in, Brainshark's programme is a great example of how a company can create, harness and amplify the advocacy of its customers to the benefit of their business and offers lessons for others looking to do the same.

HOW TO USE IT

Customer referrals don't always just happen and often customers need a bit of help and support if they are to make good referrals. One way this can be done is by building a customer advocacy programme. During our interview, Joan provided a set of top tips for firms that are interested in getting started on creating their own champion programme. They were:

- Figure out where your advocates/champions are and what they are doing.
- Segment your advocates and potential champions and understand what would be valuable to them.
- Set up a system of rewards that is aligned with the profiles and preferences of your potential champions.
- At the same time, develop and launch an employee champion programme and integrate the two.

PART 2

THE BUSINESS PERSPECTIVE

SECTION 6

COMMUNICATE

INTRODUCTION

Surveying and gathering feedback from customers is done by most businesses but, unfortunately, many don't do it very well. The reason behind this is that surveys are often designed and delivered to primarily benefit the business and do not take the customer into account. This is a shame. But, more importantly, delivery of a poorly designed customer survey or a customer feedback process can have disastrous consequences and can undo much of the good work that a business has done in delivering its customer experience. Therefore, this section will include some key insights on what it takes to successfully communicate with, survey and gather feedback from your customers and will share a number of insights, case studies, interviews and tips covering a range of issues surrounding this topic. They will include why businesses should always be honest about the length of their surveys, why always feeding back and reporting on the results of surveys is important, when is the best time to survey your customers, why you should be careful when interpreting customer feedback data and how timing your surveys pays all sorts of dividends.

INSIGHT 52 BE HONEST ABOUT YOUR SURVEYS AND KEEP THEM SHORT

Use this when you want to implement a more effective way of asking customers for their feedback.

Asking customers for feedback is an essential part of the learning and improvement process for any business and most companies do now ask for feedback. However, many who work so hard to deliver great service and build up trust with their customers undo a lot of their great work through their surveys and feedback process.

For example, have you ever received a call or an email asking you for feedback about a recent purchase saying that it would just take a few minutes only to discover that the 'few minutes' invariably turns into a lengthy series of questions, many of which feel completely irrelevant?

I have and I'm sure you have too. Guy Letts of CustomerSure, a customer feedback and follow-up software firm, provided an extreme example, during an interview,[1] when he told a me about a time he stayed at a mainstream hotel and after being there for seven hours the hotel sent him a feedback survey that was 53 pages long: 53 pages!

These sorts of practices often leave customers feeling annoyed and slightly duped as a firm's desire for feedback on everything that is important to them overtakes what is appropriate and important in the eyes of their customers.

OpinionLab, a provider of Voice of Customer listening solutions, conducted some research[2] that supports this idea. They found that:

- 80% of customers have abandoned surveys that they see as being too long.
- Less than 14% of customers are willing to spend more than 5 minutes on completing a feedback form.

So, if you are going to ask your customers for feedback then, first, be honest with them about how long your survey will take to complete and, two, keep your surveys as short as possible. This is only common courtesy and doing so is likely to protect the relationship that you have built up with your customer.

INSIGHT IN ACTION

A couple of years ago I was returning from a rock-climbing trip to Mallorca with a bunch of friends. It was a great trip with lots of laughs and some fantastic climbing.

However, on the plane on the way back the air crew distributed a customer satisfaction/feedback survey and asked the passengers to complete it and return it to the crew before they disembarked.

I looked at this questionnaire and it was five pages long and very detailed. This caused me some concerns and I wondered how many passengers would complete such a survey. I looked around the cabin and saw many passengers receive the questionnaire, look it over and then, turned off by its length, place it in the pocket in the chair in front of them.

Personally, I completed a small part of the survey and then went to hand it over to one of the cabin crew. As I did that, I then asked how these surveys went down with their passengers and what sort of response rates they got. The stewardess I asked replied that they didn't get many responses as it was too long but they continued to distribute it as they were targeted on distributing the feedback form as part of their performance reviews. This was despite the fact that they had informed senior management how customers felt about the survey and had recommended that they make it shorter.

What is clear is that this travel company is missing a great opportunity to get more feedback from its customers but is not willing to put the effort into make their surveys shorter.

Why is it that senior management ignore feedback from frontline staff about things not working and don't implement recommended changes? Is it that it is too hard? Is it to do with internal data needs, politics and culture? How does it impact the relationship with the customer?

HOW TO USE IT

Many customers want to give firms feedback but often the way that firms ask for feedback gets in the way. Here are some key tips on how you can get the most out of your customer surveys.

TIPS

Keep your surveys short: If you want to maximise response rates then make sure that your customers don't have to spend more than 4–5 minutes maximum in completing your survey. In practical terms, this could mean keeping the number of questions in your survey to around three or four, particularly if you are asking customers more open-ended questions that require a written response. If you are just asking a series of multiple choice or rating questions then keep your number of questions to no more than seven or eight.

Only ask questions that are relevant to the customer: Firms when designing surveys often succumb to the temptation to sneak questions into surveys that are not relevant to a specific transaction or experience. Resist the temptation. Customers will notice if you are focused and will thank you for it.

Try asking for written feedback: Most surveys tend to be made up of rating scales and multiple choice questions. However, this approach can tend to be biased to what you think the customer considers important or what you consider is important. Consider asking your customers open-ended questions where they have a chance to provide feedback in their own words. This way you'll find out their real opinion and what's really important to them.

INSIGHT 53 ALWAYS FEED BACK AND REPORT ON RESULTS

Use this to understand the importance of always reporting back results of any feedback received.

I often get a chance to speak to business owners and executives who are surveying their customers and when I do I ask them what they have gone on to do with the results. That's where I get various responses like:

- 'Good question!'
- 'We packaged up the results and sent them out to the team.'
- 'We presented findings to the Board.'
- 'We were quite happy with our customer satisfaction numbers as it hit our targets so we haven't done anything else.'
- 'We haven't done anything with the results yet.'
- 'We're happy with the way the numbers are.'
- 'We have no plans.'
- 'We're thinking about what they mean for our business.'

Do you see a problem with these responses?

Isn't asking for someone's opinion and then not doing anything substantial with it or not telling them what you are going to do following their input disrespectful? Would it have been better not to ask at all? How would you feel if someone kept asking for you opinion but never told you how that opinion had helped?

Well, it seems like this sort of behaviour is quite common as research into European companies by Customer Champions[3] shows that:

- 95% of companies ask their customers for feedback and measure levels of satisfaction.
- 50% take the results from the feedback and communicate it to their employees.
- 30% analyse the results, decide what they are going to do about it and create an action plan.
- 10% set up teams and allocate resources to implement their action plans.
- Only 5% of companies communicate their plans to their customers.

Follow up and follow through on any feedback process is a real issue for many firms and the risk is that by not following up or providing feedback to the customers you have surveyed you risk damaging the relationship that you have with them. However, going further than most and completing the feedback loop is also a big opportunity and one where firms that do so stand out amongst their competitors and build stronger and more open relationships with their customers.

INSIGHT IN ACTION

One company that specialises in helping firms capture feedback and use it to drive service improvement is CustomerSure. In an interview[4] with Guy Letts, founder and Managing Director of CustomerSure, he offered these insights on getting the most out of your customer feedback process.

GETTING THE MOST OUT OF YOUR FEEDBACK

Customer feedback is different from a customer review. Reviews have limited use as a tool to drive business and service improvement.

Feedback systems are generally designed to benefit the business and do not make the experience useful for the customer.

Guy believes that firms should flip their approach around so that the customer benefits. In turn, the business will accrue benefits with interest.

Simple and short is a good rule of thumb to adopt when designing a customer feedback survey.

Focus on generating actionable feedback not statistics and response rates.

Don't send reminders to customers about completing your feedback form as that's not to their benefit. That's all about your company. If your customer can and they want to give you feedback, they will.

Even now, whilst there may be a lot of feedback generated from customers much of it goes to the wrong people and it isn't collated, disseminated, distributed to the right people or acted upon. This can often leave customers with live problems feeling ignored.

So, make sure you deliver feedback to the right operational teams that can fix the problem.

Feedback should act as a warning system for a business to take care of and fix their customers' problems. This should happen first and before any analysis is done or any service improvement initiatives are started.

Customers aren't saved by analysis and averages but rather by specific direct action in a very timely way.

Better service drives sales and improvements in your business in ways that you won't understand until you start to ask your customers.

In Guy's 30 years of experience, customer feedback is unquestionably the single most effective way of improving the financial performance of a business.

HOW TO USE IT

Many firms ask for feedback but few follow through and do anything about it. Fewer still take action based on the feedback and only a very few actually report back to their customers what they have done with their feedback. As a result, closing the feedback loop is a huge opportunity that is missed by many firms.

Here are a few questions that will help you figure out what you are doing right and where you need to work harder. Whenever you answer 'No' then that's where you should be starting:

- Are you asking your customers for feedback in a way that makes sense for them and is quick and easy?
- Are you disseminating the results to your employees?
- Are you identifying individual problems and acting quickly to resolve them?
- Are you analysing the results and making action plans to drive business improvement?
- Are you putting the right people and resources in place to implement your action plans?
- Are you feeding back the results of the feedback and what you plan to do about them to your customers?
- Finally, are you updating your customers on the progress that you are making?

INSIGHT 54 # WHEN'S THE BEST TIME TO SURVEY YOUR CUSTOMERS?

Use this when you need to understand when is the best time to ask customers for feedback.

Many companies diligently survey their customers and work hard at doing it well. They also aim to keep the disruption for the customer to a minimum by using methods like Net Promoter Score (NPS) or Customer Effort Score (CES).

That's all great.

However, many get the timing wrong and fall into the trap of surveying too early, too late or they try and survey too many things at the same time.

In addition, in some cases it's not clear what is being surveyed . . . the service received in selling and delivery of the product or service or the use of the product or service itself. Surveying both at the same time can be confusing, and it may damage the customer relationship and create a missed opportunity.

I think that if companies took the time to better understand their customer's journey, they would gain better insight into the experiences they are delivering and where they should be concentrating their survey efforts. That would help them garner higher response rates from the surveys they send out and get better feedback, and it may generate more opportunities for them to stay in touch with their customers.

Let me give you an example.

Imagine I buy a bed from a high street or internet retailer. Now, most big furniture items like beds are made to order so, as customers, we would normally buy from the store, be informed of the waiting time, and then arrange a delivery date. Right?

What I have often seen happen after the company delivers the bed is that the delivery driver sends a message to operations or customer service that the bed has been delivered. In turn, the customer service department will then dutifully send out a customer feedback survey, usually by email.

That's where the problems arise. Often what happens is that the customer will get asked about their purchase experience, their delivery experience and how they like the product. However, they bought the product weeks ago, the bed has only just been delivered and they may not have slept on it much yet, if at all.

I've seen this happen many times across a range of industries where companies survey their customers and ask them the wrong questions or too many questions at the wrong time.

More often than not this is done for the company's convenience, i.e. one email or survey is easier to organise than two or three. That's just lazy and speaks volumes about how much time and effort you are willing to put in to listen to and learn from your customers.

So, make your surveys more relevant and useful by asking yourselves when is the right time to survey your customers and about what?

INSIGHT IN ACTION

In an interview,[5] Dr Mark Smith, CEO and co-founder of ContactEngine, a software firm, offers a great insight into how one company benefited from surveying its customers at the right time:

- ContactEngine uses various channels to help large firms, including Virgin Media and Wickes, contact their customers with a view to improving their customer experience.

- One of their applications helps firms communicate better with field service teams or mobile workforces and also allows them to communicate directly with customers interacting with those field service teams to solve the problem of appointment confirmation.

- There is a general rule of thumb that says that 10% of all service appointments, whether it is broadband installation or the delivery of a bag of sand or a doctor's appointment, fail.

- The reason that most appointments fail is because people forget.

- This has huge cost implications for firms with large mobile workforces and can have a significant impact on the customer experience.

- Therefore, they have worked with clients to help them communicate with their customers via various channels (text, email, web, video, apps, TVs, etc.) in the run up to appointments to make sure that they don't forget about the appointment and that it takes place.

- This has resulted in two things:

  1 A dramatic reduction in the 10%, huge efficiency gains and cost savings.

  2 It makes the client's customers happy.

- The technology also provides notifications that the appointment has taken place which then triggers a survey following the completion of the appointment to gauge a customer's satisfaction, etc.

- Most companies when following up with their customers post transaction or post appointment do so after a significant time delay.
- However, the longer the delay the more likely the customer will forget the good experience they had and it increases the likelihood that negative experiences are remembered and reported.
- When Contact Engine first started surveying their clients' customers straight after appointments they expected a 10% response, which is not a bad response rate given the normal single-digit response rate that most surveys achieve.
- However, given that they are surveying very close to the experience they have been able to achieve between 50% and 75% response rates. However, they are not just receiving ratings, like NPS scores, but they also get a huge amount of verbatim feedback.
- Therefore, given that, on average, something goes wrong with 3–5% of all transactions that gives them great insight into what goes wrong, when it goes wrong and a great opportunity to quickly solve the problem.
- Moreover, the verbatim feedback is also being used in two other areas:
  1 Helping to manage the performance of field service engineers as well as the identification of possible training requirements.
  2 The identification of individual innovations or opportunities that can be rolled out across a business. Mark uses an example of the gas boiler engineer who shows up with a piece of red carpet to put under the boiler to catch any dirt or bits whilst he is working – this has now been rolled out and is called the 'red carpet treatment'.

HOW TO USE IT

The old saying 'timing is everything' is spot on and very relevant when it comes to asking for customer feedback. To get better results from your customer surveys by improving their timing, you should consider doing the following:

- Map your customer journey and understand where your customer surveys fit into that.
- As in the examples above, consider if you are asking the right questions at the right time?

- If not, amend your surveys to make sure you are only asking for the most appropriate feedback at the best time.

- Too often firms send our surveys in batches to large numbers of customers. That might be convenient and make sense for the business but it may result in a significant delay between some interactions and any survey reducing the impact and relevance for the customer. To get better results, move your surveying approach away from batch and/or mass surveys to one that is linked to individual transactions or service interactions.

INSIGHT 55   BE CAREFUL WHEN INTERPRETING DATA

Use this as a warning about the dangers of misinterpreting feedback from customers and what to do about it.

Gathering feedback data is one thing but analysing it and understanding what it means can be a very different thing. Understanding the data and what it means can be difficult and requires specialised skills.

Research[6] by the Aberdeen Group, a business intelligence research firm, found that when businesses get it right and use advanced analytics skills and tools they benefit from a:

- 10.5% boost in annual revenue growth;
- 8.1% annual boost in customer satisfaction; and
- 5.1% decrease in annual service costs.

However, get it wrong and misinterpret the data, particularly the context in which it has been given, and it can prove very costly. Just look at the problems that Tesco have faced in recent years. Although they have been able to accumulate masses and masses of data through their ClubCard programme, their slip from a position as the leading UK supermarket has been attributed[7] to misinterpreting their data and the evolving needs of their customers.

Also, more recently, they have considered selling[8] the data mining part of their business. That does not necessarily mean they have fallen out of love with data. Rather, it just means they have been burnt and now want to adopt a back to basics approach as they seek to recover their 'mojo' and get back on track.

INSIGHT IN ACTION

A year or so ago I attended a customer service event about the future of the contact centre. At the event one of the speakers, let's call him David, told a story about what happened when he called his bank's customer service facilities.

David started his story by saying that if he was to rank his relationship with his bank he would rate it, on average, as a 5 out of 10.

However, on this occasion, he called the bank, his call was answered quickly and his problem was solved without much fuss. So, at the end of the call, when asked to rate his experience he gave it a near perfect 9 out of 10.

What happened next is the most interesting bit.

As a result of his call rating, the bank started sending messages to him believing that he was now a '9 out of 10' customer, happy with his bank and that he was now primed to recommend the bank to all of his friends, family and everyone in between.

However, the problem is that David is still, on average, only a '5 out of 10' customer when it comes to how he feels about his bank and his 9 out 10 rating was only for his experience relating to that call. Moreover, the more messages that he received from his bank treating him as a '9 out of 10' sort of guy, the more the bank annoyed him.

Surveying your customers and asking them to rate their experience with you is a good thing and a great way to gauge how you are doing. And, it's always exciting to achieve scores like 9 out of 10 when you are trying to deliver a great customer experience. But, we have to be careful not to jump to any conclusions when we achieve a big jump in positive customer feedback and we must remember to look at the result in its wider context. In David's case, the bank mixed up how he generally felt about his bank with his rating of his most recent service experience. Extrapolating a view of your customer based on one data point is dangerous, and it can back-fire and do more harm than good to your relationship with your customer.

Relationships can change dramatically overnight, as a result of one new experience, but it doesn't happen very often. Therefore, we need to be careful with the use and interpretation of data.

HOW TO USE IT

Be careful about interpreting your customer data and make sure that you understand the context in which it was given.

However, with the proliferation of data becoming available to companies these days there is another challenge ahead. Vivek Jetley, Senior Vice President and co-Head of Analytics and Head of Corporate Strategy at EXL, suggests in an interview[9] that a 'skills gap' exists and firms will struggle to find the right skills to help them analyse, interpret and action insights from the data that they gather. He goes on to say that the skills gap tends to fall into two or three broad brackets:

- The data scientists – people who can do advanced analytical and statistical work. Vivek estimates that the skills gap for data scientists in the US and UK is around 300,000–400,000 people.

- The bigger gap lies with managers – those with the right amount of training and understanding that can take, interpret and decide how to use the product of the data scientists' work. Vivek estimates that this gap is 3–4 times that of the gap for data scientists.

- The next gap lies with people that have consumer behaviour and process understanding who can help manage the implementation of data insights into the various customer channels. Vivek estimates this gap to be in the region of another 200,000–300,000.

Therefore, to maximise the value and insight that you gain from the data that you gather be prepared to hire specialist skills. However, be aware that these sorts of skills can be hard to find so start your search for the skills that you need early.

SECTION 7

MOTIVATE

INTRODUCTION

When designing great service or experience the impact of the employee is often overlooked or pushed down the priority list. The fact is that great customer experience is designed, delivered and underpinned by great people and a great culture. This section aims to put your people at the centre of your thinking about your customer experience and will include key insights on what it takes to successfully generate the sort of culture and employee engagement that underpins any effort to deliver world-class customer experience and customer service, as well as some of the issues that surround its measurement and improvement. The insights will include why it's important not to over-engineer your culture but to keep it simple, the link between customer experience and employee engagement, why engagement is not something that is done to people, what it takes to be the best when it comes to employee engagement and why you should design your employee experience.

INSIGHT 56 WORK HARD AND BE NICE TO PEOPLE

Use this to help articulate a simple and compelling culture statement for your business.

Peter Drucker,[1] the famous management thinker, professor and author, is widely attributed as saying:

Culture eats strategy over breakfast.

These words are frequently quoted by people who see culture at the heart of all great companies, particularly those ones that are lauded for their customer service and being able to deliver a consistently excellent customer experience. Companies like John Lewis, Southwest Airlines, Nordstrom and Zappos.

However, in many cases culture, like strategy, when implemented often suffers from 'over-engineering' or becoming so complicated that any culture change programme or initiative becomes its own barrier to success.

What leading companies have learned is that there is value and power in keeping your culture and values as simple as possible.

INSIGHT IN ACTION

One fast-growing UK company success story that typifies this approach is Hawksmoor, a rapidly growing restaurant brand in London and Manchester.

In an industry that is typified by high staff turnover and low levels of employee engagement the fact that Hawksmoor was voted No.12 in the Sunday Times 100 Best Companies[2] to work for in 2015, up from No. 21 in 2014, is testament to their approach and what they have achieved.

Will Beckett, founder of Hawksmoor, believes that their customer service and success is driven by happy people all striving for the same high standards. A key element of that is Hawksmoor's culture, which they describe as: 'Work hard and be nice to people.'

Will, in an interview about their culture,[3] goes on to say that:

- Hawksmoor encourage their staff to embrace their individual personalities as they will then be happier at work and create a friendlier and better environment for customers.
- Hawksmoor are aware that many people are not happy at work and tend to have to 'change' when they 'clock in' to become 'professional' versions of themselves. They then revert back to their

real selves when they leave. Hawksmoor go the other way and invite their employees to come to work and be a good version of themselves.

- That means that each table in their restaurants gets a slightly different customer experience dependent on the waiter/waitress but the standard of service they receive will be the same.
- This has helped Hawksmoor attract and retain great people, many of whom are often very individual characters that other hospitality businesses wouldn't have hired.
- Will believes that Hawksmoor's primary role is to make sure that their staff are happy and their staff's primary role is to make sure that the customers are happy.
- Finally, Hawksmoor believe that if they find people that can 'work hard and be nice to people' then they can pretty much teach them everything else.

HOW TO USE IT

Simplifying your culture, like Hawksmoor has done, is not easy but it is worth the effort.

To do that, here are a few things that you can do to help.

TIPS
Consider replicating, modifying or plain copying Hawksmoor's culture statement if it works for your business.
If not, find and articulate your own simple culture statement but make sure that it's no longer than 7–10 words in length.
Match your culture statement with a set of standards that you want your employees to strive for.

Alternatively, consider implementing an organisational constitution as suggested by Chris Edmonds[4] where:

- An organisational constitution is a set of rules that makes values and citizenship as vitally important to the organisation's success as results and performance.
- The four elements of an organisational constitution are:
  1 purpose (what you do, for whom and to what end);
  2 values and behaviours;

3 strategy; and

4 goals.

- Chris says that firms that have implemented an organisational constitution have seen boosts to customer satisfaction and employee engagement in the region of 40% as well as profit increases of 35% or more.

For more detail, check out Chris' book, *The Culture Engine: A Framework for Driving Results, Inspiring Your Employees, and Transforming Your Workplace.*

INSIGHT 57

THE LINK BETWEEN CUSTOMER EXPERIENCE AND EMPLOYEE ENGAGEMENT

Use this to understand that high employee engagement underpins great customer experience and what indicators you can use to better understand how engaged your workforce is.

Designing and delivering great service and a great customer experience is not just about technology, process and systems – it's also about people. Not people that come to work and just clock-in and then clock-out, but people that care about what they do, care about their customers and care about what their company stands for.

These are the engaged.

However, research[5] by Gallup in 2012 found that only 30% of all employees in the US, only 17% in the UK and, on average, only 13% of employees worldwide are really engaged with what they do at work. What's more worrying is that Gallup has been conducting this research since 2000 and the figures have not altered very much in that time.

But, additional Gallup research shows that when firms do work hard to create, build and develop a highly engaged workforce they significantly outperform their peers across a number of relevant metrics. For example, their research[6] shows that firms with a highly engaged workforce experience:

- 37% less absenteeism;
- between 25% and 65% lower staff turnover, depending on the industry;
- up to 41% fewer quality issues;
- 48% fewer safety incidents;
- 28% less shrinkage;
- 10% higher customer ratings;
- 21% higher productivity; and
- 22% higher profitability.

Moreover, research[7] by Temkin Group published in their 2015 'Employee Engagement Benchmark Study' also found that companies that had a market-leading customer experience had 50% more engaged employees than the majority of their competitors.

But, what is engagement? And, what does an engaged employee look like?

Well, definitions of engagement abound and you only have to conduct an internet search for 'What is employee engagement?' to come across numerous similar but also slightly different definitions.

What we can say is that engaged employees come in all sorts of shapes and sizes but, typically, they will tend to be passionate, enthusiastic, positive, creative and they are willing to go the extra mile to do their job and drive the business forward. Also, more often than not they are more likely to be emotionally connected to the purpose of the business and their work.

Whoever they are and whatever they look like, what is clear is that engaged employees are one of the key elements in building a successful and thriving business. They are also the bed-rock of getting things done and delivering a great customer experience.

INSIGHT IN ACTION

One company that really gets employee engagement and is reaping the benefits is Pets At Home. In an interview,[8] Ryan Cheyne, former People Director at Pets at Home, offered some insights into what they have done to develop their levels of employee engagement in their business and how it has benefited them:

- Pets At Home came first in the Sunday Times Best Big Companies to Work For in 2013 after coming second the year before.
- However, for them taking part in The Sunday Times competition was only used as an indicator of how they were doing on their journey to become a truly amazing place to work.
- Employee engagement is at risk of becoming an HR term that will go out of fashion. But, in actual fact, it is a 'long game' and it has taken Pets At Home eight years to get to where they are now.
- Employee engagement for Pets At Home is about having a business that is full of people that are really 'up for it', passionate about what they do, understand how what they do fits in with the big scheme of things and are real advocates for the business.
- Central to delivering that are the following three things:
  1 Recruit the right people.
  2 Train them and give them the right tools and skills they need to do their jobs well.
  3 Reward and recognise them.

- When they started, they had no data to support or underpin what they were trying to do. It just felt like the 'right thing to do'. It was a 'leap of faith'. However, eight years on they have endless amounts of data that supports the business benefits of their chosen strategy.

- These are not tricky or complicated things to do but, when you are dealing with people, they take time to filter through and to start to work.

- Whilst 92% of their employees are pet owners it's not a prerequisite to work for Pets At Home. However, one of the key characteristics they look for when hiring people is that they 'get' pets as they understand that not everyone has the right personal circumstances to be able to have a pet.

- But, they also know that not all those that 'get' pets are good with people and are willing to do the hard work that is involved with being in a retail environment. Therefore, that's the balance that they strive to identify in the people who they hire.

- Their model, as per the Service Profit Chain,[9] is that if you recruit the right people and create a great place to work they will deliver great service to their customers and that will put money in the till.

- They also know that when employees in their stores are most engaged, their customer feedback scores tend to be higher and their customers tend to spend more per transaction.

- When Ryan joined the business their staff turnover was over 70% and they were spending over £300,000 a year on recruiting new retail management. Now, they have more than doubled their number of stores and they only spend £30,000 a year on recruitment costs because their staff turnover has plummeted.

- Whilst many people might deride this as being 'soft', Ryan believes (and their data and performance backs this up) that whilst delivering the soft stuff is often hard it also delivers hard results.

- One of the most powerful, long-lasting and impactful ways to recognise people, they have found, is hand-written notes.

- Once they had become No. 1 on the Sunday Times list they decided not to enter again and are now looking to challenge themselves even more and continue to learn by benchmarking themselves against other amazing places to work like Southwest Airlines, Apple, Google and Zappos.

- Finally, this is all about realising their vision of becoming the best pet store in the world and an amazing place to work.

HOW TO USE IT

To deliver a great customer experience requires great people. How great they are will depend on how engaged they are with your business and what you are trying to achieve. However, before you commission an employee engagement survey and to get a quick insight into how engaged your team are you need to gather data on the following indicators:

- level of absenteeism;
- staff turnover;
- participation in meetings;
- projects getting completed on time;
- team members coming up with new ideas;
- team hitting targets.

Once you have gathered the data ask yourself these questions:

1 What sort of picture do they paint of the health of my business?
2 How do they compare to other firms in my industry or other firms around me?

These indicators aren't perfect but they will give you a good idea of the levels of engagement that exist within your business.

After all, it's about what gets done rather than what gets said. Isn't it?

INSIGHT 58 # ENGAGEMENT IS NOT SOMETHING THAT IS DONE TO PEOPLE

Use this to help you understand and identify the real drivers of your employees' level of engagement.

Often when firms discover or realise they have an employee engagement problem, one of the first things they do is commission an employee feedback survey. Alternatively, they may look to acquire a set of 'tools' that will help drive improvement of their company's employee engagement.

In fact, if you do a search for 'employee engagement', amongst the different definitions you'll find all sorts of links and pointers to surveys, tools, programmes and strategies that will help you improve your employee engagement.

That's all good stuff.

But, if you look at the research, particularly the Gallup research into employee engagement,[10] you will discover that the quality of managers explains 'at least 70% of the variance in employee engagement scores'.

Therefore, we can conclude that employee engagement is not something that is done to people. In large part, it's a function of what your managers do and how they behave.

INSIGHT IN ACTION

In an interview,[11] Kevin Kruse, bestselling author on the subject of employee engagement[12] and a former partner of Kenexa (acquired by IBM in 2012), a leading player in the employee engagement space, offered some additional insights on how to create an engaged workforce:

- Engagement is something that managers and employees do together rather than something that is done to employees. It is a collaborative, two-way conversation with both sides having an obligation and a responsibility for their own contribution.
- Kevin talks about the 3 P's of the career-life bull's eye:
  1 passion (what do you like doing, what gets you out of bed, what you like having fun with);
  2 purpose (where do you want to serve, in what area do you want to make a contribution); and
  3 pay (what can you earn a living doing, what standard of living do you want to achieve).

- Kenexa's research shows that over 70% of engagement (how one feels at work) is driven by three things:
  1 growth (personal and professional challenge);
  2 recognition (a feeling that you are appreciated); and
  3 trust (which is not just ethics but that the employee trusts that the future is bright).
- Employee engagement surveys when done right can identify the areas that need work. When done wrong they are just cosmetic and a waste of money and resources.
- However, engagement surveys are not the be-all and end-all and changes in managers' behaviour that focus on growth, recognition and trust can generate much greater returns.
- How you treat your employees will have a direct effect on how they treat your customers . . . common sense that is not so common.
- Employee engagement does drive better business results. Kenexa's research shows that publicly traded companies with the most engaged employees, i.e. those in the top 25%, outperform the bottom 25% in terms of share price performance by 500%.
- One of the challenges that many companies face is that the type of leadership, management and culture that is required to create an engaged workforce (or an engaged customer base, for that matter) is foreign to many executives. Particularly, those who came up through the ranks when companies were solely organised on military/industrial-type command and control structures, where they managed tasks and managed people as resources.
- Employee engagement is really driven by the relationship that an employee has with their boss.
- The problem in a nutshell: Most of us are managers of tasks rather than leaders of people.
- The challenge is how can we become more mindful of our role every day as a leader of people rather than a manager of tasks.
- One piece of advice for all managers: Get out from behind your computers and spend more time with your people.

HOW TO USE IT

When facing an engagement problem, many businesses assume that more and better internal communications or more surveys will increase engagement. They might. But, there are no guarantees with those types of initiatives.

Syed Hasan, CEO of ResponseTek, a customer experience software solution provider, in an interview[13] sums up the customer experience and employee engagement picture when he says:

- You can't design a great customer experience only at the senior level of the business.

- You can't design a customer experience and expect it just to be great, you have to engage the front-line employees and get them involved.

- Reasonable compensation, an interesting job and a voice in an organisation seem to be the keys to employee engagement. Most companies focus on the first two but don't do the last one and that is where the real value is. Employees have a lot to contribute and that is key to getting their full engagement.

However, giving your employees a voice in the organisation is not the only thing that firms need to concentrate on. A number of studies[14] have shown that there are several drivers of employee engagement. In general, their results can be boiled down to the following.

DRIVERS OF EMPLOYEE ENGAGEMENT
The need for good immediate management.
Two-way communication that is listened to, responded to and acted upon.
Effective team work and cooperation.
Receiving recognition for a job well done.
Allowing employees to have an impact on their organisation (i.e. listen to their views and act on them).
A leader, manager or supervisor who encourages and helps people to develop themselves and their career.

A role that allows the employee to do what they do best.

Regular feedback on how they are doing whilst also asking how you (as managers/leaders/supervisors) are doing.

Leadership that really cares for employees.

Friendly and helpful team-mates.

Having the necessary tools and resources to perform well.

These drivers provide a clear 'to-do' list for companies that want to improve their employee engagement.

How does your firm perform against all of the elements on that list?

INSIGHT 59 # DESIGN THE EMPLOYEE EXPERIENCE TOO

Use this to help design an employee experience that is aligned with the customer experience that you want to deliver.

Throughout the book, we've established that to deliver a complete and great customer experience you need to map it out, design it, deliver it and then keep adjusting it in order to keep improving.

We've also established that to deliver a great customer experience requires great employees.

But, according to the International Data Corporation (IDC) 2015 Experiences survey,[15] whilst 81% of firms report that they use customer satisfaction surveys to measure their customers' satisfaction and experience nearly 70% of them don't measure their employees' experience.

So, how do they know that they are doing a good job of managing them or if they could do better?

Therefore, as in the case of customers, if firms want to find, recruit, nurture, develop and retain great employees then they would do well to think about designing their employee experience too.

INSIGHT IN ACTION

Jo Taylor, former Director of Talent Management at Talk Talk, agrees and thinks that companies miss a trick if they don't design a compelling employee experience. In an interview,[16] she elaborates and says:

- Employees now want an experience.
- Rewards (which is not just about money) and recognition are really key ways of driving the employee experience and allowing a 'high-touch' culture to develop.
- Companies need to remember that they are selling to two groups: their customers and their employees.
- Many companies miss a trick when they outsource their job application sites to third parties and save money by not branding the third party site.
- What makes a really great place to work is the people and how you unlock the potential that exists within those people.
- Everyone in the organisation has the keys and opportunity to contribute to that goal.

- However, many firms focus too much on the top 100 in their firm and how they manage the business. In the process, they neglect the majority of their employees where most of the work, culture and customer contact takes place.

- Jo believes that employee experience should mirror what happens when a company launches a new product or service and should have three stages: pre-life, early life and in-life experience.

- Like designing a new customer experience, companies should be designing their employee experience and should focus on how they can make that experience as good as possible so that the employee is engaged, sure that they have made the right choice to work for that firm and are then committed to doing a good job.

- Many companies spend a lot of money on the in-life experience and very little in the pre-life stage.

Henry Stewart, author of *The Happy Manifesto*[17] and CEO of Happy, a training and consultancy company, extends the concept and adds a 'post-life' element. In an interview,[18] he says that:

- In their firm they don't part on bad terms. When they fall out with people (it doesn't happen very often), they don't sack people straight away. Their approach is to help them move on to their next project. This means that even if they have had to part company with someone they still talk positively about the company.

- The best bit about this approach is that it makes recruitment very easy. Happy has a 2,000 long waiting list of people wanting to work for them. The last time they needed new trainers or associates, there was no advert, no recruitment consultant, no external cost at all. All that was required was one email to their waiting list which resulted in 92 applications and the recruitment of three new employees.

HOW TO USE IT

It makes no sense that you wouldn't apply the same rigour, approach and tools that you would do if you were designing your customer experience to designing your employee experience. If you don't design it then aren't you leaving a large element that underpins your customer experience to chance?

If you haven't yet designed your employee experience, start with a journey mapping exercise like you would do if you were designing your customer experience but this time put your employee at the centre of the exercise.

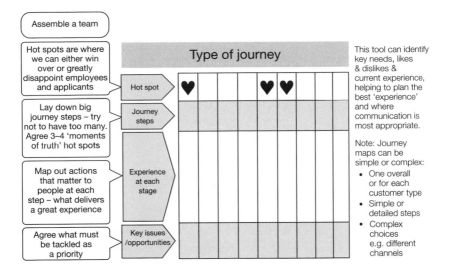

Use a slightly modified journey mapping tool (or the diagram) to help you map it all out and then implement it.

Doing so will significantly increase your chances of attracting, recruiting, developing and retaining great employees.

SECTION 8

LEAD

INTRODUCTION

L eadership is key to any organisational endeavour and delivering world-class customer experience and customer service is no exception. Leaders have to consider what is the right course of action, what is the right organisational structure, how they can respond to competitive developments as well as thinking about how they can stay ahead of their competitors and aligned with their customers. At the same time, leaders have to think about how they too can develop so that they can lead their teams and develop the right culture that will underpin any world-class customer experience. Leaders don't have it easy. Therefore, this section will offer some insights into the issues leaders should consider when creating and delivering excellent customer experience. The insights will include whether leaders should consider changing their organisational structure to improve customer experience, how they can change their organisation to become more agile and responsive to their customers' needs, how systems thinking can offer a route to transforming customer service and customer experience, why turning measures into targets can be dangerous, how to move the organisation away from a target-based performance culture to more of a behavioural model, as well as some individual leadership lessons.

INSIGHT 60

WHAT'S THE BEST ORGANISATIONAL STRUCTURE TO DELIVER YOUR CUSTOMER EXPERIENCE?

Use this to help question and review your organisational structure and ask whether it is the best one to deliver the customer experience that you desire.

Over the years we have seen many different variations in company structure with businesses organised by specialism, function, market, geography, matrix, etc.

However, following significant changes in markets, competition, customer behaviour and preferences, and technology in recent years some of the more traditional, and particularly functionally-based, structures are now being called into question. The criticism of these structures ranges from they are not agile or responsive enough, they are way too siloed and thus limit collaboration, all the way through to complaints that they are no longer fit for purpose and don't match the needs of the modern marketplace, customer base and workforce.

As a result, there has been and continues to be lots of innovation and discussion around what is the best organisational structure to deliver the best outcomes for customers and businesses alike. As a result, many organisations are experimenting with or moving to alternative structures including structures like:

- holacracy,[1] as used by Zappos, a company much loved by its customers and employees;
- a team-based, flat, lattice organisation[2] as used by W. L. Gore & Associates, whose mission[3] is 'To make money and have fun' and who as well as delighting their customers are continually ranked in the US and UK as one of the best companies to work for;[4] and
- democratic organisations[5] as used by the publicly traded WD-40 Company, manufacturer of the eponymous WD-40 lubricant, whose stock price (at the time of writing) has grown by a factor of four in the last six years and who on their 2104 employee engagement survey achieved an engagement score of nearly 94%.[6]

So, what is the best organisational structure for your business?

Some people will argue that form should follow function. But, does it? Maybe success criteria, rather than function, should determine the form of your organisation.

The real answer to 'What is the best organisational structure for your business?' is: it depends. It will depend on your market, your customers and your people. However, what is clear is that it is no longer sufficient to assume that a traditional, functional-based structure is the best way to go.

INSIGHT IN ACTION

Here's a great example of a firm, G Adventures, that has radically changed its organisational structure to allow it to engage its employees and customers more effectively.

G Adventures, the world's largest, small-group, adventure travel company, are a leader in their niche and have been delivering double-digit growth year on year for the last 20 years. They also operate in 100 countries, generate over $170 million a year in sales and have over 2,000 employees.

In an interview,[7] Bruce Poon Tip, founder of G Adventures, told me that:

- Traditional business focuses on profitability and growth first and then works backwards from there. In their (*Looptail*)[8] philosophy, they focus on their people and their culture first and the rest falls into place.

- Their structure addresses the changes that are happening around them and allows their customers and employees to become their biggest brand advocates.

- The HR function has been eliminated from G Adventures as Bruce believes it is there to control and 'manage' the bottom performing 10% of your people as a company grows. However, it also stifles performance so was eliminated.

- Bruce has dropped the title of CEO (Chief Executive Officer) as he wanted to make sure that the traditional CEO position was not the most important position in the company.

- The most important position in the company is the customer-facing employee. Therefore, each customer-facing employee in G Adventures has the title Chief Experience Officer (CEO) . . . and there are hundreds of them.

- This has helped employees make a mental shift to become more customer and externally focused.

- It has also helped bring them together, particularly as a team that is spread out over 100 different countries.

- Bruce gets the most pleasure from the stories that come from the partners and children of some of his employees, when they tell him how the work that they do, their organisational structure and their purpose has had such a positive and lasting impact on their personal and family lives. That does not mean that they are doing different jobs, it's more that they are now working for a company that they believe in and that stands for something more than profits.

- The book (*Looptail*) that Bruce wrote tells the story of G Adventures and their transformation. It is meant to act as an internal document as well as a book for public consumption.

- The foreword was written by, and the book has been endorsed by, His Holiness The Dalai Lama, who has never endorsed a business book before.

- In essence, what they have done is move away from a traditional, hierarchical structure to one that is flatter and more 'circular' in nature. This is designed to help them keep leadership at the centre of decisions but, at the same time, helps create enough freedom amongst their employees so that it drives sustained innovation, great results as well as engaged employees and customers.

Because their system is based on 'circles' it has been compared to the 'holacracy' approach. However, in the 'holacracy' approach a company organises itself around the work that needs to be done and not around people occupying specific job functions.

HOW TO USE IT

Just because you've historically organised your business a certain way doesn't necessarily mean that is the way you should always organise things. Organisations have to adapt to their environment as much as anything else if they are to survive and prosper.

However, given the example above, this doesn't mean that every firm should be thinking about 'circles' when they consider what the right organisational structure is for them and what they want to achieve.

Leaders need to ask themselves the following questions about their organisational structures.

QUESTIONS ABOUT ORGANISATIONAL STRUCTURE

Is your organisation flexible enough or nimble enough to be able to respond quickly to changing market and customer demands?

Does your organisation suffer from siloed working?

Are your silos getting in the way of effective and efficient collaboration and cooperation across your organisation?

Are your departments and functions working well enough together in order to deliver the best customer experience?

If not, what do you need to do?

Could changing your organisational structure help you improve your customer experience?

INSIGHT 61

BECOMING MORE AGILE AND RESPONSIVE TO CUSTOMER NEEDS

Use this when you need to help your organisation become more agile and ready to respond to ever-changing customer needs.

A firm's ability to become more 'agile' and more responsive to customers' needs is seen as an increasingly important source of competitive advantage.

But, talking about being agile and actually becoming more agile and responsive are two very different things.

A series of discussions[9] with a number of leaders and senior executives in the customer service and experience space identified some of the barriers that firms need to overcome if they are to become more agile.

BARRIERS TO OVERCOME

Alignment: The senior team all need to be focused on delivering the same objectives and be aligned to the brand and customers rather than their own departments.

Complexity: As a company gets bigger it becomes more complex. Firms need to fight that complexity at every juncture.

Different customer relationships: Companies will have customers that are at different points on their customer lifecycle and, thus, they will have different relationships with them. These all need to be managed carefully.

Lack of understanding of customers: Even now, many companies struggle to understand their customers, their needs and who their ideal customer is.

Lack of understanding of the marketplace: Despite continuously changing and challenging market and competitive conditions, many firms are still coming to terms with how their markets have changed and what to do about it.

Fear of change: Change is never easy and many resist it due, in some part, to fear – fear of the unknown, fear of the speed of change, fear of competition, fear of the customer, etc. Fear, however, if not managed, can often lead to paralysis.

INSIGHT IN ACTION

Alan Trefler, Founder and Chief Executive Officer of Pegasystems, in an interview[10] builds on this and suggests that:

- Companies that don't commit to agility and customer centricity could face a 'customerpocalypse' and risk getting torn apart or abandoned by their customers.

- It's amazing how quickly firms can now move from positions of dominance or success (e.g. Nokia and Blackberry) to positions of destruction or desperation.

- Only if you learn to look at your business differently will you be able to build a business that can thrive in the future.

- Do it well and you'll not only improve customer engagement but you'll also simplify the business and save money at the same time.

HOW TO USE IT

Organisations need to become more agile and responsive to customer needs if they are to continue to prosper. For some that will mean a new organisational structure. For others they will conclude that their current organisation is fit for purpose and will focus on other challenges like alignment, complexity, understanding and dealing with change.

In the face of these challenges, I then asked the same series of leaders what companies should be doing in their quest to become more 'agile' and more responsive to their customers' needs. They came up with the following five tips.

TIPS TO BECOME MORE AGILE AND RESPONSIVE

Joined up working and thinking: Mark Lancaster, CEO of SDL, suggests that organisations need to connect up their siloed functions so that they work more in a joined up way. This is not a panacea but giving employees this as well as a platform to share and exchange information is a good first step.

Understand the impact and manage it: Jim Dicso, President of SundaySky, suggests that firms would do well to first define what putting the customer at the centre of their business really means. Leaders then need to understand and manage the impact of any proposed changes.

Constant stream of incremental improvements: Charlie Peters, Senior Executive Vice President of Emerson, suggests that firms should focus on incremental and constant change rather than transformational change. He says that customers benefit from a constant stream of incremental improvements that preserves those elements of product or service which they historically value. Improving customer service, therefore, probably involves evolution rather than transformation.

Improve speed of decision making: David Lloyd, President & CEO, Intelliresponse, suggests that firms should focus on improving their decision making and how they make decisions so that they can make the process as swift and nimble as possible. He advocates that analysis and decision making should be iterative – taking lots of minor decisions in a short period of time – which also helps manage excessive risk.

Get rid of fear by building self-awareness: Kevin Kelly, author of *DO! The Pursuit of Xceptional Execution*, cites a 2007 *Harvard Business Review* article[11] which found that the most important attribute for modern leaders to develop was self-awareness. He suggests that senior management teams need to work on building their self-awareness as a way of recognising, managing and overcoming any 'fear' that exists in the boardroom. Only then will boards have the confidence in themselves and each other to navigate the complex and ever-changing challenges that lie ahead.

INSIGHT 62 # UNLEARNING OLD WAYS CAN HELP TRANSFORM CUSTOMER EXPERIENCE

Use this when you are considering how you can transform your organisation, move to new ways of working and in the process deliver excellent customer service.

With things around us changing so fast, a key skill and driver of successful organisations and their leaders is being able to adapt.

However, in reality, adaptation requires that organisations must make choices; choices to stop doing certain things in order to be able to do new things. This is often not easy as it can require challenging, questioning and abandoning historical norms or ways of doing things. In order to do this, we often have to 'unlearn' old ways of doing things before we can learn and adopt new ways of operating.

INSIGHT IN ACTION

One firm that has successfully unlearned the way they approach service and customer experience is Aviva. In an interview[12] with Rob Brown, former Systems Thinking Director at Aviva, he explained more about what they have done:

- The problem they had to solve was to figure out how to make their customer service more efficient.

- However, they found that whatever they did their service got worse.

- So, they resolved to try and do something different and they started their 'unlearning' journey in 2008 by using a method called 'systems thinking'.

- They used The Vanguard Method,[13] as pioneered by John Seddon. This required them to forget about how they traditionally operated their business and focus only on what matters to customers, removing anything that isn't of value to customers.

- To achieve this, they worked with their front-line staff to identify problems and then make the necessary changes and improvements to their service.

- As a result, many back-offices procedures were moved into the hands of front-line staff so that they could directly attend to and solve customers' problems as and when they occur.

- Doing so has allowed them to reduce complaints, reduce the number of customers calling back and improve customer satisfaction, whilst also reducing operational costs by tens of millions of pounds.

- Aviva piloted this approach in the pensions area of their business. Where this approach has been implemented customer satisfaction has improved significantly and is now in the region of 80–90% and employee morale/engagement which was below 50% is now at 70%.

- Rob notes that, historically, Aviva believed that giving customers whatever they wanted was expensive. But, in fact, they have found that the opposite is true and giving customers what they want in the way that they want it is far more efficient and better for the business.

HOW TO USE IT

Change is hard at the best of times. But change that requires us to look at the way we do things differently and 'unlearn' our old ways is especially hard. However, taking on and succeeding at the challenge can bring great rewards.

For leaders that are interested in exploring how systems thinking can benefit their business, John Seddon, pioneer of the Vanguard Method, in a follow-up interview[14] suggests the following to get you started:

TIPS

If you have regular calls coming into your business, in a call centre say, then go and listen to a number of those calls.

For each call that you listen to, ask yourself if this call is:

- **value demand,** i.e. an enquiry from a customer about something they want that is for their benefit (e.g. renewing a subscription, ordering a new product or service, increasing an order or providing some feedback); or

- **failure demand,** i.e. an enquiry from a customer about something that has come about due to the business's failure to do something or do something correctly (e.g. faults with products or services, problems with a delivery, a mistake on an invoice, non-receipt of a contract, a customer's question wasn't resolved the first time they called, the customer not being able to find the answer they were looking for on the company's website).

Doing so will give you an idea of what service issues are a function of what the business is doing or, rather, not doing right.

Following that the next thing you should do is establish whether the 'failure demand' that you have identified occurs regularly and is predictable.

If it is regular and predictable then you can make a plan to alter and improve your system to eliminate future instances of that failure demand.

Doing so will free up your customer service representatives to concentrate on delivering the things that are of value to the customer.

INSIGHT 63 USING BEHAVIOURS RATHER THAN TARGETS TO IMPROVE YOUR CUSTOMER EXPERIENCE

Use this when you need to transform your organisation and adopt new behaviours that put the customer at the heart of everything that you do.

For a long time, targets have been used to help businesses, teams and individuals focus on and drive performance improvement. And for many businesses and roles they work well.

However, some targets, if they are not set well and not thought through, can drive the wrong sort of behaviour and work against the organisation, its customers and the delivery of a great customer experience.

Consider the example of Swinton,[15] one of the UK's largest high street insurance retailers, that was fined £7.3 million by the UK's Financial Conduct Authority (FCA) in July 2013 for mis-selling to and mistreating customers. The FCA attributed this to their very aggressive sales strategy and targets around add-on insurance products as well as accusing them of not providing customers with enough information and key terms of their insurance policies.

As such, many organisations are starting to recognise the negative impact that targets can have on a business's culture and how this impacts the customer experience, and are starting to move towards performance structures that are more focused on behaviours and measuring customer satisfaction rather than sales targets.

A great example of a company leading the way in their industry comes from Lookers, a large car retailer with 120 dealerships in the UK that sell around 140,000 new and used cars a year. In an interview[16] with the *Telegraph* in August 2015, CEO Andy Bruce says that:

Lots of people feel as if they are walking into a lion's den when they walk into a car showroom, that's the image the industry has created for itself.

To change that image and develop the right culture and the sort of behaviour that goes with it, Lookers are piloting new pay schemes that do away with the traditional car sales wage structure of low basic salaries plus commission. They are replacing them with much higher basic salaries with any performance or variable element to be based on customer satisfaction.

INSIGHT IN ACTION

Here's another example of a firm that is moving away from a target-based performance culture that they found got in the way of putting the customer first and delivering a great customer experience.

The business in question is the Principality Building Society, a Welsh building society founded in 1860 and head-quartered in Cardiff. Principality is the largest building society in Wales and the sixth largest in the UK. In an interview,[17] Damian Thompson, Director of Distribution at Principality, explains how they transformed their customer experience and culture by moving away from targets towards behaviours:

- Their objective is to move away from an individually based performance culture to one that looks at what behaviours support customer service and differentiation of their organisation.
- At the heart of this is how they ask their customers for feedback.
- In most organisations, feedback is requested and sent out by head office and often there is a significant time lag between the customer's experience and when the survey is sent out. Moreover, the results of feedback often take an age to reach the person who has served that customer last.
- As a result, Principality have empowered colleagues who have served the customer to ask for feedback immediately following an individual's experience. They also ask for suggestions on what customers think they could improve on.
- Doing that has been the cement around which they have built a more customer focused organisation.
- Moreover, when that feedback comes back into the business it can be seen by everyone across all of their channels, offices and branches.

EXAMPLES OF CHANGES MADE ON THE BACK OF CUSTOMER FEEDBACK

One customer came into a branch with her elderly mother and told them via their feedback process that none of the chairs in their branches had holds, or arms on them, that her mother could use to help her get up out of the chair (her mother had bad knees). As a result of that feedback being shared around the organisation, the branches came back and suggested that they put one chair (i.e. with arms) in every interview room that would be suitable for elderly customers with a similar condition. That suggestion was agreed and implemented overnight.

When customers go into a branch for an appointment, which may be an hour or two hours long, they are offered a cup of tea or coffee. In many organisations, that would normally be tea or coffee from a vending machine. But, it's not the same quality as tea or coffee you would make at home. Customers notice this and mention it too in their feedback. So, Principality started making 'real' tea and coffee also ensuring that they sourced the materials from the local shops. This small tactic has generated a huge number of compliments.

- Principality have now extended their transformation programme and to facilitate knowledge sharing they have developed an internal forum where colleagues share ideas about things that they have done and changes that they have made: what has worked and what hasn't.
- This has allowed them to promote a culture where they celebrate and reward not only the customer service 'heroes' that deliver great service but also the ones that share great stories from within the business or from other businesses.
- Damian believes that you can boil the success factors of their transformation down to three things:
  1 Self-regulation – where people are encouraged to continuously learn as they did when they were children.
  2 Outside-in – they encourage employees to notice and share things that they do or see inside their branches that could help their other colleagues. They also encourage them to share what they have seen or experienced, with regards to great service, outside of Principality that they think the organisation could learn and benefit from.
  3 Speed of action – how they can do more of the good things and less of the bad things as quickly as possible.
- The results that they are getting are very good. For example, their NPS is very strong, they achieve customer satisfaction scores of 88% and their employee engagement scores are around 90%. In addition, they are achieving around 50% response rates on their customer surveys.
- They are securing further benefits by closing the feedback loop with their customers and are telling them: 'You told us this and we've done it.'
- They are two years into their transformation programme and Damian believes that it will be another two before he will be comfortable that the organisation and his colleagues are 'on the path'.

Moving to this type of culture poses lots of challenges for leaders and the three things that leaders need to consider are:

1 Set a realistic time-frame as it's not going to happen overnight.

2 If you want to put the customer at the heart of your organisation then you need to physically find a way of doing that.

3 Be clear with individuals and teams about how working together can benefit the customer.

HOW TO USE IT

We have seen that performance targets if not carefully considered can drive the wrong sort of behaviour and can, in fact, jeopardise a business's ability to deliver excellent service and a great customer experience. Many firms now realise this and are moving away from a target-based performance culture to one that is more focused on encouraging the sort of behaviour that underpins great service and experience.

Damian offers the following tips to transform your organisation from a target-based culture to one that is based more on behaviours that put the customer at the centre of your business:

TIPS

Utilise people from outside your industry: Go and look for best practice and work out how you can implement it in your business. But, be aware that you may not have to go far afield to find what you are looking for as the insight and best practice that you are looking for may come from your local take-away restaurant or hairdresser.

Be brave: What you will be attempting may not be the norm in your industry so make sure you have the strength to see it through.

Plan appropriately: Changing behaviours does not happen overnight so don't make promises that you can't keep.

If you do these things and execute your plan brilliantly then you will have a really good chance of success.

INSIGHT 64 LEADERSHIP BEHAVIOURS AND CUSTOMER EXPERIENCE

Use this to help you understand that your own behaviour, as a leader, has a huge impact on both customer experience and employee motivation and what you can do about it.

A friend of mine sent me an article that he had found on LinkedIn. The article,[18] 'Why everybody should think they are the Chief Customer Officer – reflections on building a customer focused business' was written by David Thodey, who at the time was the outgoing CEO & Executive Director of Telstra, Australia's largest telecoms and media company.

In the article, David reflected on the progress that Telstra have made 'to put the customer at the centre of everything we do' and the lessons that they have learned along the way.

David listed out his first lesson as 'Leaders need to show a genuine commitment' and goes on to explain that:

> Leaders need to be seen talking to and about customers, asking questions, listening to their stories, making a difference. Real change comes from real actions.

However, how many leaders in firms are, actually, performing 'real actions'? In other words, how many leaders are 'walking the talk'? How many are out talking to customers on a regular basis, listening to their problems, helping them, serving them and making a difference to them?

These actions offer two clear benefits:

1 They allow CEOs and leadership teams the opportunity to listen, learn and experience directly what their customers and their employees go through on a daily basis.

2 It turns their words into real actions and demonstrates to their customers that they really care and do put them at the heart of everything they do. In turn, it's likely to inspire and motivate their staff to do the same too.

INSIGHT IN ACTION

Another great example comes from Craig Newmark, founder of Craigslist, who routinely introduces himself as the company's customer service representative.[19] He regularly interacts with his customers, listens to them and when they complain he himself is ready to fix the problem. His actions speak volumes about his desire to create a customer-centric business.

But, this sort of practice is not that common.

For example, when was the last time that you saw:

- a leader of an oil and gas firm spending time at one, or a number, of their petrol or filling stations serving or just talking to their customers;
- a train company leader checking tickets on the train or at a station;
- a member of the leadership team at a big software company accompanying one of their sales reps on a regular sales meeting/call; or
- the CEO of a retail bank taking deposits, speaking to and helping customers in a local branch.

Why does this not happen more regularly? Is it to do with the 'distance' that has been created between CEOs, senior management and their frontline employees? Is it to do with culture? Is it to do with how we organise our work and our organisations? Is it to do with a perceived 'best use of my time' idea?

Shouldn't spending more time directly with and helping your customers be right at the top, or near the top, of every boss's list?

HOW TO USE IT

It's not enough anymore to tell a good story about customer experience. As the old saying goes 'Actions speak louder than words'. Therefore, leaders need to understand that if they want to transform the customer experience of their business then they need to reduce the 'distance' that exists between them and their frontline employees and their customers.

To understand what they need to do next, leaders should ask themselves the following questions:

- When was the last time that I was 'on the tools' delivering work for my customers or sitting side by side with my employees serving customers?
- Do I know what it's like to do the job of my frontline employees? Not intellectually but viscerally?
- When was the last time I observed my customers? Talked to them directly, without it being a contrived, managed or set-up situation?
- When was the last time that I 'experienced' my own customer experience? And, did I really see things as a customer does and use my own money?

Answers to these questions will give you a good idea of the 'distance' that exists between your position and role and what you need to do next.

INSIGHT 65 HUMILITY AND THE BENEFITS OF ADMITTING THAT YOU GOT IT WRONG

Use this to help you understand that as a leader you don't always have to get it right and there can be real benefits behind getting it wrong, admitting when you have done so and then putting it right.

Everything is changing . . . customer behaviour and expectations, competition, technology, how we organise our businesses, etc. However, what about leadership? Does it need to change in the face of these new demands?

Ted Coiné and Mark Babbitt, authors of a 2014 book, *A World Gone Social,* think it does and in an interview[20] they suggest leaders need to be a lot more open, nimble and accountable to their customers and their stakeholders and not just their investors.

This needs humility and requires them to step up and acknowledge when there is a problem or when a mistake has been made, and then to state what they are going to do to fix it.

Obviously, how people react will depend on the size and nature of the problem. But, assuming that the problem hasn't caused serious harm, customers recognise that leaders are human and respect the fact that they are acknowledging the problem, taking responsibility for it and resolving to fix it.

Many leaders and companies have found that doing so has allowed them to generate more trust, more respect and more value from their customers.

INSIGHT IN ACTION

A great example of this comes from Ryanair and their CEO, Michael O'Leary. In an exclusive interview[21] with the *Daily Mail* in October 2014, Michael O'Leary admitted that: 'We should have been nicer to customers earlier than we have been.'

This from a man who, in the past, had been known to call customers 'stupid' and has mused publicly about whether they should 'charge customers to go to the toilet' amongst other things, as they relentlessly pursued a cost leadership strategy.

I explored this change of heart with him in an interview[22] when he told me that:

- Despite low prices working very well, some customers didn't like what Ryanair were doing, e.g. free seating or charging for an additional cabin bag. So, they changed that and are embarking on a series of other measures to change/remove the things that their customers don't like.

- They have decided to listen to their customers and make changes where it doesn't impact on the cost base.
- Humility is the biggest lesson he has learned in the last 12 months, even if as he says, 'It's very difficult for someone who is Irish to be humble. We generally believe that we walk on water.'

Listening to customers has been a 'spectacularly successful learning experience for Ryanair over the last 12 months' and they are seeing the changes that they have implemented reflected in their business results too.

Do as much as you can to be nice to your customers but stay true to your business model. Ryanair know that service and improving their customers' experience is good but only as long as it doesn't threaten their cost leadership position. Investing in being nicer to customers should fuel and add to your strategy but shouldn't dominate or replace it.

As he mentioned, admitting their mistakes, doing so publicly and making the right sort of changes is really benefitting them. In March 2015, Ryanair announced that:

- They carried 6.7 million passengers in March 2015, up from 5.2 million in the same month the previous year, representing a 28% jump.
- Their load factor (the airline industry's measure of how full planes are) also jumped over the same period from 80% to 90%.
- Over the same period, Ryanair's share price grew by more than 43%, as profits and passenger numbers have continued growing.

HOW TO USE IT

What is clear is that it is Michael O'Leary's humility and ability to admit that he has made mistakes that are the main driving forces behind Ryanair's customer service improvements.

But, there are lessons for leaders facing similar challenges.

A 2015 report by the Said Business School, the University of Oxford, and Heidrick & Struggles,[23] captures the situation well when it states:

Sometimes you have to have the courage to say, 'I know this is the right direction,' the humility to say when you've got it wrong and deal with it, but the courage to take action when you believe it's the right thing to do – despite the downside potential for yourself.

WHEN A MEASURE BECOMES A TARGET, IT CEASES TO BE A GOOD MEASURE

Use this to help you understand that converting a performance measurement metric into a target is not always wise and is not guaranteed to generate the results that you want.

Goodhart's Law[24] states that:

When a measure becomes a target, it ceases to be a good measure.

It is named after Charles Goodhart, a former member of the Bank of England's Monetary Policy Committee and Professor at the London School of Economics, and it first appeared in a 1975 paper on monetary policy. Originally only applied to monetary policy it grew in popularity and is now applied in many other areas, particularly in the setting of targets and measuring of performance in organisations.

For example, consider the case of Sears, Roebuck and Company in the 1990s, described in a 2011 article in the *Harvard Business Review* called 'Ethical Breakdowns'.[25] The organisation wanted to increase the speed of repairs and, as such, the management set its mechanics a sales goal of $147 per hour as a way of increasing throughput.

However, rather than increasing the speed of repairs, what happened was that the mechanics started overcharging customers and 'fixing' things that weren't broken in order to meet their new sales target.

Whilst the management's goal of increasing the speed of repairs is understandable, we can see that by translating a performance measurement into a target ended up promoting the wrong sort of behaviour from their mechanics and the wrong sort of results.

INSIGHT IN ACTION

EXAMPLES OF THIS LAW IN ACTION

Can you recall a time when you called a call centre seeking help for an issue or problem that you had and during the call you sensed that the agent wanted to speed things up or wanted to conclude things as quickly as possible as you got towards the end of the conversation? If you have, then the organisation that you were calling is probably using 'call time' as a performance target rather than as a measure. Yes, monitoring the time that agents spend on the phone answering customers' queries can be a useful gauge of how long it takes to solve certain queries and how agents are performing. However, when an organisation takes that measure and translates it into a target, particularly if it is a 'stretch' target, then that can often have a negative impact on service and satisfaction as it focuses the agent more on finishing the call in time rather than delivering the best service or experience for the customer.

Contrast the above example with what Zappos, the internet retailer and doyen of customer service, do.[26] Zappos do track call time but don't use it as a target as they prefer to focus on encouraging their Customer Loyalty Team members, as they call them, to focus on doing what is right for their customer. Therefore, they expect their team members to spend 80% of their time helping customers. But, most importantly, they are not concerned with how many customers they help in that time, it could be 1, 10 or 100. What they believe is that if they focus on helping their customers it will encourage repeat custom and, in turn, the growth of their business. And it's working too. Founded in 1999 and focused, initially, on selling shoes, they grew incredibly fast over the next ten years and in 2008 they were profitable and generating $1 billion in gross merchandise sales annually.[27] Moreover, 60% of their buyers were estimated to be repeat customers and around 43% of their customers were estimated to come from word of mouth recommendations.[28] Further, in 2009, the company was bought by Amazon for $1.2 billion but continues to this day as a separate company (**www.zappos.com**). Jeff Bezos, Founder and CEO of Amazon, in a video statement on the acquisition said:[29] 'We see great opportunities for both companies to learn from each other and create even better experiences for our customers.'

HOW TO USE IT

Given the impact and insight of Goodhart's Law and the examples above, here are a few things that leaders should ask themselves when thinking about performance measurement and targets:

- What business objectives am I trying to achieve?
- What do I use in my business to measure service and experience?
- What's important to my business in a customer service or experience context?
    - Customer satisfaction?
    - Customer effort?
    - Ease of doing business?

- A customer's propensity to recommend your business to another person they know?
- Solving a customer's problem first time and every time?
- The time it takes to respond to a customer query?
- The time or the number of interactions it takes to resolve a customer's query?
- The reasons that customers call?
- The utilisation rate of my customer service representatives?
- The satisfaction and engagement of my customer service representatives?
■ Are my targets and performance measures aligned with those?
■ Are they driving the right sort of behaviour?
■ What is the consequence of those targets in terms of the customer's experience?

Measures, targets and metrics will differ across businesses and industries but the key is to pick measures and targets that relate to your business objectives and ones that matter to your customers.

INSIGHT 67   WHAT HAVE YOU DONE TODAY TO MAKE THE LIVES OF YOUR TEAM EASIER?

Use this question to continuously review and identify where you can help your team improve their performance by focusing on them and making their jobs easier.

Do you, your management, your culture or your organisational and administrative requirements help or hinder employees to do their job?

If you ask most leaders and managers whether they or their organisation help or hinder their employees they will invariably answer: 'We help.'

However, just because leaders, managers and organisations think they are helping does not necessarily mean that it is true.

Research into what employees spend their time doing at work paints a very different picture. For example, a survey,[30] by AtTask in 2014 found that employees at large US firms only spend 45% of their time on doing the work that they were hired to do, i.e. their main responsibility that would be laid out in their job description. The other 55% of the time is taken up by things like sending, responding to and sorting emails, unproductive as well as useful meetings, administrative tasks and interruptions.

These results are not unusual. What they do, however, is call into question many of the things that are done in organisations and whether they actually hinder productivity and the performance of employees and your business.

So, leaders and managers would do well to consider what they can do or what they should stop doing so that they can make the lives of their teams easier.

INSIGHT IN ACTION

Peter A. Hunter, a leading authority on employee engagement and author of *The Problem With Management – and How to Solve It,* in an interview[31] tells an interesting and relevant story about helping employees do their jobs better:

- Much of Peter's experience and his stories come from his time working in the Navy, particularly with Polaris and Trident submarine missile crews.
- He recalls a time when he was put in charge of a number of very experienced people and he quickly figured out that there was no way that he could tell them what to do as they knew much more about

the work than he did. Rather, he realised that the best way for him to operate was to find out what they needed to complete their work and then get it for them.

■ He realised that by creating the environment where his team were responsible for themselves they took pride in what they did.

■ Peter suggests that the problem with management is that it was ever called management. If it was instead called facilitation then we would have a completely different idea of what management is about and what it entails.

■ Many managers tell people what to do because they are threatened by people showing initiative.

■ However, people, generally, want to show up for work and do a good job. They want to be proud of what they do. They want to use their education, creativity and imagination to do work that they are proud of.

The culture we want to create already exists. We just need to let it happen.

HOW TO USE IT

Too often managers, leaders and organisational bureaucracy and practices get in the way of people doing their jobs, being productive and performing to the best of their abilities. Therefore, if managers and leaders want to get more out of their team, raise their productivity and their engagement, get out of their way and, in turn, enable them to focus on delivering great service and an excellent customer experience they should ask a series of questions.

They should ask their employees and teams:

■ What should we be doing more of?

■ What should we be doing less of?

■ What do we do that gets in the way of you doing your job?

Following that, they should then ask themselves this question on a regular basis:

What have I done today to make the lives of my team easier?

The answers to these questions will produce the ideas that will help you focus on and start to make your environment and organisation better.

INSIGHT 68　DON'T BELIEVE THE HYPE

Use this to help you understand that there is no technology silver bullet and that you would do well to focus on the present and what is important now.

The business environment is becoming more and more complex due to rising competition, new and disruptive entrants to markets, changing customer behaviour and expectations and the growth in the number of channels that firms can use to communicate with their customers.

This is further complicated by the rapid advances and promise of new technology from things like:

- big data;
- the Internet of Things (IoT);
- virtual intelligence;
- predictive analytics;
- voice of the customer;
- virtual reality;
- wearable technology;
- machine learning;
- speech to speech translation, etc.

All of these have mooted applications for customer service and customer experience.

However, when it comes to technology business leaders would do well to recognise and keep in mind that new technological developments are often surrounded by a lot of promise and even more hype.

Yes, technology can do some amazing things but we need to be careful that we do not focus on what could possibly happen and lose sight of what will probably happen. Also, in the midst of the hype we need to be wary that in our efforts to improve 'customer experience' we don't lose sight of 'the customer's experience'. If we do we run the risk of failing to live up to our own and our customers' expectations.

INSIGHT IN ACTION

A useful bellwether of emerging technology comes from Gartner, a US information technology research and advisory firm. For the last 20 years they have been producing Hype Cycles,[32] which provide insight into the position of numerous types of new technologies across five stages of development (Innovation Trigger, Peak of Inflated Expectations, Trough of Disillusionment, Slope of Enlightenment and Plateau of Productivity).

However, through research and monitoring the emergence of different technologies for business applications they have found that:[33]

> *fundamental advances in technology are still taking over a decade – sometimes up to 30 years or more – to traverse the Hype Cycle from initial prototypes to mainstream adoption.*

This does not mean that technology cannot move from emergence to hype to adoption faster but businesses would do well to view new technology with some caution. For example, Gartner has also found that:

- Cloud computing was first identified as a technology to watch in 2009 but it is only now that firms are starting to realise its full potential and it is moving towards becoming a mainstream technology.
- Wearable computers/technology were first identified as an emerging technology in 1997 but it has still to achieve significant traction and adoption.
- Businesses and technologists have known and talked about the benefits and possible applications of speech recognition since 1995 but it took until 2013 for Gartner to recognise that it had reached wide-scale adoption and productivity.
- Finally, virtual reality has been talked about for years but has still not fulfilled its potential and is stuck in what Gartner calls its 'Trough of Disillusionment'.

HOW TO USE IT

Firms should always consider how technology can help them attract, engage, serve and retain their customers now and how it may help them do a better job in the future. However, they should also realise that technology may not be the 'silver bullet' that its hype suggests.

Getting caught up in what could happen and what might be runs the risk of distracting you from something that delivers real value to your business and is of value to your customers now.

Therefore, in the midst of rapidly evolving technology, leaders would be wise to:

- Stay present but keep an eye on the future.
- Focus on the whole journey.
- Keep things simple.

- Anticipate problems.
- Realise that consistency is paramount.
- Focus on the little things that matter.
- Deliver what customers want and value.
- Make things easy for your customers (and employees).
- Realise that everyone matters.
- Add a little extra from time to time.
- Use technology wherever you can to help.

But, most of all, leaders would do well to disbelieve the hype.

FINAL WORDS

I hope that you have enjoyed these insights and can see where you can apply some of them in your business. It's not an exhaustive list and will develop over time.

However, I would like to devote the final word of this book to a dream that I have.

It's a bit tongue in cheek and idealistic, perhaps. But, I have a dream that if every business in the world improved their customer service and customer experience just a little bit, then we could make the whole world a bit better. People would get better customer service and a much improved customer experience which would make them happier and because they are happier there would be fewer problems and they'd get into fewer arguments. If fewer arguments took place then there would be fewer disagreements, fewer fights and less conflict. And as the ripple effect spread it could contribute towards achieving world peace.

It's a dream.

But, are you with me?

What did you think of this book?

We're really keen to hear from you about this book, so that we can make our publishing even better.

Please log on to the following website and leave us your feedback.

It will only take a few minutes and your thoughts are invaluable to us.

www.pearsoned.co.uk/bookfeedback

NOTES

INTRODUCTION

1 The British Museum. Available at: <**http://www.britishmuseum.org/ research/collection_online/collection_object_details.aspx?objectId=2777 70&partId=1&searchText=WCT53297&page=1**>

2 Oracle, 2011. *2011 Customer Experience Impact Report.* [pdf]. Available at: <**http://www.oracle.com/us/products/applications/ cust-exp-impact-report-epss-1560493.pdf**>

3 Echo, 2011. *2011 Global Customer Service Barometer.* [pdf]. Available at: <**http://about.americanexpress.com/news/docs/2011x/ AXP_2011_csbar_market.pdf**>

4 Walker. *Customers 2020.* [online] Available at: <**http://www .walkerinfo.com/customers2020/**>

5 Watermark Consulting, 2015. *The 2015 Customer Experience ROI Study.* [pdf]. Available at: <**http://www.watermarkconsult.net/docs/ Watermark-Customer-Experience-ROI-Study.pdf**>

6 Forrester. *Customer experience professionals.* [online] Available at: <**https://www.forrester.com/Customer-Experience**>

7 Kriss, P., 2014. The value of customer experience, quantified. [online] *Harvard Business Review*. Available at: <**https://hbr .org/2014/08/the-value-of-customer-experience-quantified/**>

8 Swinscoe, A., 2014. *Quantifying the business value of a great customer experience – interview with Peter Kriss of Medallia.* [online] Available at: <**http://www.adrianswinscoe.com/ quantifying-the-business-value-of-a-great-customer-experience- interview-with-peter-kriss-of-medallia/**>

SECTION 1

1 McKinsey & Company, 2014. *Innovating automotive retail.* [pdf]. Available at: <**http://www.mckinsey.com/~/media/McKinsey/dotcom/ client_service/Automotive%20and%20Assembly/PDFs/Innovating_ automotive_retail.ashx**>

2 Government Communication Service. *Insight exploration: customer journey mapping.* [pdf]. Available at: <**https://gcn.civilservice.gov.uk/ wp-content/uploads/2013/02/customer-journey-mapping-diagram.pdf**>

3   Kemp, N., 2015. The content obesity epidemic. [online] *Marketing*. Available at: <http://www.marketingmagazine.co.uk/article/1348565/bad-strategy-creating-content-obesity-epidemic>

4   Warc, 2015. *Consumers 'tune out' marketers.* [online]. Available at: <http://www.warc.com/LatestNews/News/Consumers_tune_out_marketers.news?ID=34973>

5   Swinscoe, A., 2013. *Customer service, people and how caring does scale – interview with Gary Vaynerchuk #1aDayQandA.* [online] Available at: <http://www.adrianswinscoe.com/customer-service-people-and-how-caring-does-scale-interview-with-gary-vaynerchuk-1adayqanda/>

6   CEB. *The digital evolution in B2B marketing.* [online] Available at: <http://www.executiveboard.com/exbd-resources/content/digital-evolution/index.html>

7   Swinscoe, A., 2012. *Inbound and content marketing may make up 80% of all marketing in the future – interview with Mike Volpe of Hubspot.* [online] Available at: <http://www.adrianswinscoe.com/inbound-and-content-marketing-may-make-up-80-of-all-marketing-in-the-future-interview-with-mike-volpe-of-hubspot/>

8   Hill, G., 2015. *The three factor reinventing customer experience design.* [online] **MyCustomer.com**. Available at: <http://www.mycustomer.com/feature/experience/three-factors-reinventing-customer-experience-design/174631>

9   Edelman, 2015. *2015 Edelman Trust Barometer: executive summary.* [online]. Available at: <http://www.edelman.com/2015-edelman-trust-barometer-2/trust-and-innovation-edelman-trust-barometer/executive-summary/>

10 Swinscoe, A., 2012. *Extreme Trust and why it's important you're your customers and your business – interview with Martha Rogers and Don Peppers.* [online] Available at: <http://www.adrianswinscoe.com/extreme-trust-and-why-its-important-for-your-customers-and-your-business-interview-with-martha-rogers-and-don-peppers/>

11 Swinscoe, A., 2014. *Customer loyalty is becoming a collective experience – interview with Steve Abernethy of SquareTrade.* [online] Available at: <http://www.adrianswinscoe.com/customer-loyalty-is-becoming-a-collective-experience-interview-with-steve-abernethy-of-squaretrade/>

12 Swinscoe, A., *Using* customer reviews to drive service improvement, WoM and growth - interview with Jan Jensen

of Trustpilot. Available at: <**http://www.adrianswinscoe.com/ using-customer-reviews-to-drive-service-improvement-wom-and-growth-interview-with-jan-jensen-of-trustpilot/**>

13 Swinscoe, A., 2013. *Outstanding brands become part of their customers story – interview with Bernadette Jiwa.* [online] Available at: <**http://www.adrianswinscoe.com/outstanding-brands-become-part-of-their-customers-story-interview-with-bernadette-jiwa/**>

14 Swinscoe, A., 2015. *Brands with purpose build better relationships with their customers – interview with Jeremy Waite.* [online] Available at: <**http://www.adrianswinscoe.com/brands-with-purpose-build-better-relationships-with-their-customers-interview-with-jeremy-waite/**>

15 TOMS. *What we give.* [online]. Available at: <**http://www.toms.com/ what-we-give-shoes**>

16 Swinscoe, A., 2012. *Want more customers? Try focusing on art, culture and greatness – interview with David Hieatt of Hiut Denim.* [online] Available at: <**http://www.adrianswinscoe.com/ want-more-customers-try-focusing-on-art-culture-and-greatness-interview-with-david-hieatt-of-hiut-denim/**>

17 Goodreads. [online] Available at: <**http://www.goodreads.com/author/ quotes/43587.Alan_Alda**>

18 Statistic Brain Research Institute, 2015. *Attention span statistics.* [online]. Available at: <**http://www.statisticbrain.com/ attention-span-statistics/**>

19 Acuna, K., 2013. *Why movies today are longer than ever before.* [online] Business Insider. Available at: <**http://www.businessinsider .com/movies-are-getting-longer-2013-1?IR=T**>

20 Carroll, D., 2012. *No customer is statistically insignificant: inside scoop with Dave Carroll.* [online] CustomerThink. Available at: <**http://www.customerthink.com/interview/ inside_scoop_with_dave_carroll**>

21 Sibun, J. and Fletcher, R., 2010. Surprise as Sir Terry Leahy resigns from Tesco. [online] *The Telegraph*. Available at: <**http://www .telegraph.co.uk/finance/newsbysector/retailandconsumer/7812463/ Surprise-as-Sir-Terry-Leahy-resigns-from-Tesco.html**>

22 Neville, S., 2014. Ex-Tesco chief Terry Leahy blames woes on successor Philip Clarke's weak strategy. [online] *The Independent*. Available at: <**http://www.independent.co.uk/news/business/news/ extesco-chief-terry-leahy-blames-woes-on-successor-philip-clarkes-weak-strategy-9834535.html**>

23 Stern, S., 2010. What men need to learn about leadership. [online] *Financial Times*. Available at: <**http://www.ft.com/cms/s/0/7d099a7c-7d5e-11df-a0f5-00144feabdc0.html#ixzz1Roay3aWr**>

SECTION 2

1 Swinscoe, A., 2011. *What makes first direct so successful – interview with their new CEO Mark Mullen.* [online] Available at: <**http://www.adrianswinscoe.com/what-makes-first-direct-so-successful-interview-with-their-new-ceo-mark-mullen/**>

2 Swinscoe, A., 2014. *Big and little data, building trust and B2B marketing – interview with Charlie Peters of Emerson.* [online] Available at: <**http://www.adrianswinscoe.com/big-and-little-data-building-trust-and-b2b-marketing-interview-with-charlie-peters-of-emerson/**>

3 Swinscoe, A., 2012. *Extreme Trust and why it's important you're your customers and your business – interview with Martha Rogers and Don Peppers.* [online] Available at: <**http://www.adrianswinscoe.com/extreme-trust-and-why-its-important-for-your-customers-and-your-business-interview-with-martha-rogers-and-don-peppers/**>

4 Edelman, 2015. *2015 Edelman Trust Barometer: executive summary.* [online] Available at: <**http://www.edelman.com/2015-edelman-trust-barometer-2/trust-and-innovation-edelman-trust-barometer/executive-summary/**>

5 Swinscoe, A., 2015. *Advocate assisted commerce improves customer experience and drives business results – interview with Scott Pulsipher of Needle.* [online] Available at: <**http://www.adrianswinscoe.com/advocate-assisted-commerce-improves-customer-experience-and-drives-business-results-interview-with-scott-pulsipher-of-needle/**>

6 Moss, C., 2013. *From the 'Apple Lisa' to the U2 iPod: Apple products that totally flopped.* [online] Business Insider. Available at: <**http://www.businessinsider.com/10-old-apple-products-that-totally-failed-2013-11?IR=T**>

7 Swinscoe, 2012. *You can't make 'Art' if you are not willing to fail – interview with Seth Godin on The Icarus Deception.* [online] Available at: <**http://www.adrianswinscoe.com/we-need-more-people-to-create-things-that-connect-with-other-people-and-make-change-happen-interview-with-seth-godin-on-the-icarus-deception/**>

8   Ignatius, A. 2013. Jeff Bezos on leading for the long-term at
    Amazon – an interview with Jeff Bezos. *Harvard Business Review*.

9   Indexed. [online] Available at: <**http://thisisindexed.com/**>

10 Hagy, J., 2011. *How to be more interesting (in 10 simple steps)*.
    [online] Forbes. Available at: <**http://www.forbes.com/sites/
    jessicahagy/2011/11/30/how-to-be-interesting/**>

11 Swinscoe, A., 2013. *How to be more interesting (and keep
    customers for longer) – interview with Jessica Hagy*. [online] Available
    at: <**http://www.adrianswinscoe.com/how-to-be-more-interesting-and-
    keep-customers-for-longer-interview-with-jessica-hagy/**>

12 UK Customer Experience Awards '15. [online] Available at: <**http://
    c-x-a.co.uk**>

13 Evening Standard, 2013. *Npower tops customer dissatisfaction
    table as prices rise . . . and so do complaints*. [online] Available
    at: <**http://www.standard.co.uk/business/business-news/
    npower-tops-customer-dissatisfaction-table-as-prices-rise--and-so-do-
    complaints-8948445.html**>

14 KPMG Nunwood. [online] Available at: <**http://www.nunwood.
    com/2013-uk-experience-excellence-results/**>

15 Knight, E., 2015. Financial services industry can't afford any more
    scandals. [online] *The Sydney Morning Herald*. Available at: <**http://
    www.smh.com.au/business/comment-and-analysis/financial-services-
    industry-cant-afford-any-more-scandals-20150107-12jm90.html**>

16 Ombudsman Services, 2015. *Consumer Action Monitor*. [online]
    Available at: <**http://www.ombudsman-services.org/downloads/
    CAMFinal2015.pdf**>

17 Swinscoe, A., 2014. *Not having contracts equalises our relationship
    with our customers – interview with John Marick of Consumer
    Cellular*. [online] Available at: <**http://www.adrianswinscoe.com/
    not-having-contracts-equalises-our-relationship-with-our-customers-
    interview-with-john-marick-of-consumer-cellular/**>

18 Consumer Reports, 2013. *Sprint sinks to the bottom of latest
    consumer reports cell-phone service ratings*. [online]. Available at:
    <**http://pressroom.consumerreports.org/pressroom/2013/11/my-entry-3.
    html**>

19 **Out-law.com**, 2015. *Survey reveals UK consumers' online privacy
    concerns*. [online] Available at: <**http://www.out-law.com/en/
    articles/2015/april/survey-reveals-uk-consumers-online-privacy-concerns/**>

20   ICO, 2015. *Consumers concerned about how their personal details are shared, survey shows.* [online] Available at: <**https://ico.org.uk/about-the-ico/news-and-events/ news-and-blogs/2015/03/consumers-concerned-about-how-their- personal-details-are-shared/**>

21   DMA, 2012. *Data privacy: what the consumer really thinks 2012.* [pdf]. Available at: <**http://www.dma.org.uk/research/ data-privacy-what-the-consumer-really-thinks**>

22   Hern, A. and Rankin, J., 2015. Spotify's chief executive apologises after user backlash over new privacy policy. [online] *The Guardian.* Available at: <**http://www.theguardian.com/technology/2015/aug/21/ spotify-faces-user-backlash-over-new-privacy-policy**>

23   Ek, D., 2015. *SORRY.* [online] Spotify. Available at: <**https://news. spotify.com/us/2015/08/21/sorry-2/**>

24   Swinscoe, A., 2014. *Moving from the era of CRM (Customer Relationship Management) to the era of CMR (Customer Managed Relationships) – interview with Geraldine McBride of MyWave.* [online] Available at: <**http://www.adrianswinscoe.com/ moving-from-the-era-of-crm-customer-relationship-management-to-the- era-of-cmr-customer-managed-relationships-interview-with-geraldine- mcbride-of-mywave/**>

25   Ctrl-Shift, 2014. *The business opportunity of personal information management services.* [online] Available at: <**https://www.ctrl-shift.co .uk/news/2014/06/26/the-business-opportunity-of-personal-information- management-services/**>

26   Reinhardt, A., 1998. *Steve Jobs: 'There's sanity returning.'* [online] BusinessWeek. Available at: <**http://www.businessweek.com/1998/21/ b3579165.htm**>

27   McDonalds, 2014. *Five brand new burgers designed by you!* [online] Available at: <**http://www.mcdonalds.co.uk/ukhome/ whatmakesmcdonalds/articles/my-burger-your-entries-put-taste-test.html**>

28   BEE. *Customer as co-creators in innovation.* [online] Available at: <**http://www.bee-global.net/news/3-customer-as-co-creators-in- innovation.html**>

29   Starbucks. *My Starbucks idea.* [online] Available at: <**http:// mystarbucksidea.force.com/**>

30   skinnyCorp. *How it works.* [online] Available at: <**https://www.threadless .com/how-it-works/**>

31 Wikipedia. *Threadless.* [online] Available at: <**https://en.wikipedia.org/wiki/Threadless**>

32 Swinscoe, A., 2013. *Deliver great customer experience by including your customers – interview with Mark Hurst of Creative Good.* [online] Available at: <**http://www.adrianswinscoe.com/deliver-great-customer-experience-by-including-your-customers-interview-with-mark-hurst-of-creative-good/**>

33 Hurst, M. and Terry, P., 2013. *Customers included: how to transform products, companies and the world – with a single step.* New York: Creative Good.

34 Oracle, 2012. *81% of shoppers willing to pay more for better customer experience, oracle research shows.* [online] Available at: <**http://www.oracle.com/us/corporate/press/1883120**>

35 Echo, 2012. *2012 Global customer service barometer.* [pdf] Available at: <**http://about.americanexpress.com/news/docs/2012x/axp_2012gcsb_us.pdf**>

36 New Statesman, 2010. *UK consumers willing to pay more for better customer service, says survey.* [online] Available at: <**http://www.newstatesman.com/technology/2010/10/customer-experience-pay**>

37 Holland, C. Estate agency clients to pay according to quality of service. [online] *Telegraph & Argus*. Available at: <**http://www.thetelegraphandargus.co.uk/business/13598845.Estate_agency_clients_to_pay_according_to_quality_of_service/**>

SECTION 3

1 Stone, A., 2012. Why waiting is torture? [online] *The New York Times*. Available at: <**http://www.nytimes.com/2012/08/19/opinion/sunday/why-waiting-in-line-is-torture.html?**>

2 Videlica, 2015. *Waiting on hold drives 12% of UK customers to defect.* [online] Available at: <**http://www.videlica.com/waiting-on-hold-drives-12-of-uk-customers-to-defect/**>

3 Maister, D., 1985. *The psychology of waiting lines.* [online] Available at: <**http://davidmaister.com/articles/the-psychology-of-waiting-lines/**>

4 Plain Language Association InterNational, 2005. *Samples of plain language rewrites and organizational change.* [online] Available at: <**http://plainlanguagenetwork.org/**>

5 Royal Pharmaceutical Society, 2015. *RPS calls for clearer labelling on sunscreens after survey reveals confusion.* [online] Available at: <**http://www.rpharms.com/pressreleases/pr_show.asp?id=2648**>

6   Fairer Finance, 2014. *The worst banks and insurers for small print revealed.* [online] Available at: <**http://www.fairerfinance.com/ press-releases/the-worst-banks-and-insurers-for-small-print-revealed**>

7   National Adult Literacy Agency (NALA), 2015. *Irish people calling for healthcare professional to use less medical jargon.* [online] Available at: <**https://www.nala.ie/news/ irish-people-calling-healthcare-professionals-use-less-medical-jargon**>

8   Dean, J., 2011. *10 ways our minds warp time.* [online] PsyBlog. Available at: <**http://www.spring.org.uk/2011/06/10-ways-our-minds-warp-time.php**>

9   Scrace, A., 2015. *Are you sitting on a customer research goldmine?* [online] Trustpilot. Available at: <**http://blog.trustpilot.com/ blog/2015/6/11/are-you-sitting-on-a-customer-research-goldmine**>; and <**http://searchengineland.com/88-consumers-trust-online-reviews-much-personal-recommendations-195803**>

10   Swinscoe, A., 2014. *Using customer reviews to drive service improvement, WoM and growth – interview with Jan Jensen of Trustpilot.* [online] Available at: <**http://www.adrianswinscoe.com/ using-customer-reviews-to-drive-service-improvement-wom-and-growth-interview-with-jan-jensen-of-trustpilot/**>

11   ClickFox, 2012. *2012 brand loyalty survey.* [online] Available at: <**http://web.clickfox.com/rs/clickfox/images/cf-survey-results-brand-loyalty.pdf**>

12   TripAdvisor, 2013. *24 insights to shape your TripAdvisor strategy.* [online] Available at: <**http://www.tripadvisor.co.uk/TripAdvisorInsights/ n2120/24-insights-shape-your-tripadvisor-strategy**>

13   Wikiquote. *Maya Angelou.* [online] Available at: <**https://en.wikiquote .org/wiki/Maya_Angelou**>

14   Swinscoe, A., 2015. *Do you know if you are irritating your customers? – interview with Melvin Brand Flu of Liework.* [online] Available at: <**http://www.adrianswinscoe.com/do-you-know-if-you-are-irritating-your-customers-interview-with-melvin-brand-flu-of-liework/**>

15   Wikipedia. *Serial position effect.* [online] Available at: <**https:// en.wikipedia.org/wiki/Serial_position_effect**>

16   Wikipedia. *Hermann Ebbinghaus.* [online] Available at: <**https:// en.wikipedia.org/wiki/Hermann_Ebbinghaus**>

17   Halliwell, J., 2013. Iceland: 'customer engagement scheme is paying off'. [online] *The Grocer*. Available at: <**http://www.thegrocer**

.co.uk/channels/discounters/iceland-customer-engagement-scheme-is-paying-off/349715.article?>

18 Moore, R., 2008. Chris Hoy an example that cyclists can be clean of drugs and still win gold. [online] *The Telegraph*. Available at: <http://www.telegraph.co.uk/sport/olympics/2604410/Chris-Hoy-proves-cyclists-can-be-clean-of-drugs-and-still-be-mean-Olympics.html>

19 Wikiquote. *Charles Mingus*. [online] Available at: <https://en.wikiquote.org/wiki/Charles_Mingus>

20 Wikiquote. *Blaise Pascal*. [online] Available at: <https://en.wikiquote.org/wiki/Blaise_Pascal>

21 siegel+gale, 2014. *Why simplicity?* [online] Available at: <http://simplicityindex.com/2014/why-simplicity/>

22 Swinscoe, A., 2015. *Behavioural science is a gold mine for service design and customer experience – interview with Nicolae Naumof.* [online] Available at: <http://www.adrianswinscoe.com/behavioural-science-is-a-gold-mine-for-service-design-and-customer-experience-interview-with-nicolae-naumof/>

23 Behavioural Insights Team, 2014. *EAST: Four simple ways to apply behavioural insights.* [online] Available at: <http://www.behaviouralinsights.co.uk/publications/east-four-simple-ways-apply-behavioural-insights>; and <http://www.behaviouralinsights.co.uk/publications/the-behavioural-insights-team-update-report-2013-2015/>

24 CX Solutions, 2015. [online] Available at: <http://www.cxact.com/>

25 Price, J., 2015. *The psychology of customer complaints.* [online] Call Center IQ. Available at: <http://www.callcenter-iq.com/customer-insights-analytics/articles/the-psychology-of-customer-complaints/>

26 Swinscoe, A., 2014. *Find and fix customer problems by hiring a Customer Advocacy Manager – interview with Carey Smith and Dave Waltz of Big Ass Fans*. [online] Available at: <http://www.adrianswinscoe.com/find-and-fix-customer-problems-by-hiring-a-customer-advocacy-manager-interview-with-carey-smith-and-dave-waltz-of-big-ass-fans/>

27 Northrup, L., 2013. *To resolve some customer service problems, just call back.* [online] Consumerist. Available at: <http://consumerist.com/2013/06/13/to-resolve-some-customer-service-problems-just-call-back/>

28   Sabio, 2012. *Research shows that one in four inbound contact centre enquiries are unnecessary or avoidable.* [online] Available at: <**http://www.sabio.co.uk/news/2012/research-shows-that-one-in-four-inbound-contact-centre-enquiries-are-unnecessary-or-avoidable.html**>

29   Dixon, M. and Ponomareff, L., 2010. Why your customers don't want to talk to you. [online] *Harvard Business Review*. Available at: <**https://hbr.org/2010/07/why-your-customers-dont-want-t/**>

30   inContact, 2013. *US consumers want today's companies to be proactive in customer service.* [online] Available at: <**http://www.incontact.com/call-center-industy-news/us-consumers-want-todays-companies-be-proactive-customer-service**>

31   Hicks, K., 2013. *6 tips to shift from reactive to proactive customer service.* [online] Customer Service Investigator. Available at: <**http://csi.softwareadvice.com/6-tips-to-shift-from-reactive-to-proactive-customer-service-0411/**>

32   Swinscoe, A., 2015. *Proactive customer service will pay back ten fold – interview with Matt Lautz of Corvisa.* [online] Available at: <**http://www.adrianswinscoe.com/proactive-customer-service-will-pay-back-ten-fold-interview-with-matt-lautz-of-corvisa/**>

33   Leggett, K., 2014. *Forrester's top trends for customer service in 2015.* [online] Forrester. Available at: <**http://blogs.forrester.com/kate_leggett/14-12-17-forresters_top_trends_for_customer_service_in_2015**>

34   IntelliResponse. Budget truck rental. Available at: <**http://www.intelliresponse.com/wp-content/uploads/2012/09/Budget_Final.pdf**>

35   IntelliResponse. *CopaAirlines.* [pdf] Available at: <**http://www.intelliresponse.com/wp-content/uploads/2014/06/Copa-Airlines-Infographic2014.pdf**>

36   Swinscoe, A., 2013. *Smart proactive customer service that delivers results – interview with Jim Dicso of SundaySky.* [online] Available at: <**http://www.adrianswinscoe.com/smart-proactive-customer-service-that-delivers-results-interview-with-jim-dicso-of-sundaysky/**>

37   Debenhams. *Your handy buying guides.* [online] Available at: <**http://www.debenhams.com/buying-guides**>

38   Swinscoe, A., 2014. *Improve customer experience by surveying your customers quickly – interview with Mark Smith of ContactEngine.* [online] Available at: <**http://www.adrianswinscoe.com/improve-customer-experience-by-surveying-your-customers-quicker-interview-with-mark-smith-of-contactengine/**>

39 Anglian Water, 2014. *Proactive notifications improves operational efficiency for England's largest water company.* [pdf] Available at: <**http://www.aspect.com/globalassets/microsite/proactive-engagement/anglian-water-cs.pdf**>

40 Swinscoe, A., 2011. *What makes first direct so successful – interview with their new CEO Mark Mullen.* [online] Available at: <**http://www.adrianswinscoe.com/what-makes-first-direct-so-successful-interview-with-their-new-ceo-mark-mullen/**>

41 Livework. *Ask the public, not just your customers.* [online] Available at: <**http://liveworkstudio.com/client-cases/vivo/**>

42 Gneezy, A. and Epley, N., 2014. Worth keeping but not exceeding. *Social Psychological & Personality Science.* [online] Available at: <**http://spp.sagepub.com/content/5/7/796.abstract**>

43 Brandweiner, N., 2012. *Broken promises and poor service the biggest customer turn-offs.* [online] MyCustomer. Available at: <**http://www.mycustomer.com/topic/customer-experience/broken-promises-and-poor-customer-service-responsible-lost-customers/14186**>

44 Clarkson, D., 2010. *Do your customers want to telephone you for service?* [online] Forrester. Available at: <**http://blogs.forrester.com/diane_clarkson/10-04-06-do_your_customers_want_telephone_you_service**>

45 Swinscoe, A., 2014. *Building customer support communities – interview with Rob Howard of Zimbra.* [online] Available at: <**http://www.adrianswinscoe.com/building-valuable-customer-support-communities-interview-with-rob-howard-of-zimbra/**>

46 Kessler, S., 2011. *How to: Create a world-class online community for your business.* [online] Mashable. Available at: <**http://mashable.com/2011/01/12/online-community-business/**>

47 Dean, J., 2014. *The emotion which lasts 240 times longer than others.* [online] PsyBlog. Available at: <**http://www.spring.org.uk/2014/11/the-emotion-which-lasts-240-times-longer-than-others.php**>

48 Verduyn, P. and Lavrijsen, S., 2014. Which emotions last longest and why: the role of event importance and rumination. *Motivation and Emotion.* [online] Available at: <**http://link.springer.com/article/10.1007/s11031-014-9445-y**>

49 Swinscoe, A., 2014. *Nearly 60% of customers will go elsewhere following a bad delivery experience – interview with Angela O'Connell of Metapack.* [online] Available at: <**http://www.adrianswinscoe.com/nearly-60-of-customers-will-go-elsewhere-following-a-bad-delivery-experience-interview-with-angela-oconnell-of-metapack/**>

50 Swinscoe, A., 2014. *Improve customer experience by surveying your customers quickly – interview with Mark Smith of ContactEngine.* [online] Available at: <**http://www.adrianswinscoe.com/improve-customer-experience-by-surveying-your-customers-quicker-interview-with-mark-smith-of-contactengine/**>

51 Dixon, M., Freeman, K. and Toman, N., 2010. Stop trying to delight your customers. [online] *Harvard Business Review.* Available at: <**https://hbr.org/2010/07/stop-trying-to-delight-your-customers**>

52 Swinscoe, A., 2014. *Should 'Net Easy' be your new customer service metric – interview with Nicola Millard of BT.* [online] Available at: <**http://www.adrianswinscoe.com/should-net-easy-be-your-new-customer-service-metric-interview-with-nicola-millard-of-bt/**>

53 The Henley Centre for Customer Management, 2015. [online] Available at: <**http://www.hccmsite.co.uk/index.html**>

54 The Net Promoter Community. *The Net Promoter Score and System.* [online] Available at: <**http://www.netpromoter.com/why-net-promoter/know**>

55 Ombudsman Services, 2015. *Consumer Action Monitor.* [online] Available at: <**http://www.ombudsman-services.org/downloads/CAMFinal2015.pdf**>

56 Eptica, 2015. *UK brands leave over half of customer questions unanswered, according to new study.* [online] Available at: <**http://www.eptica.com/mces2015_news**>

57 Wikipedia. *Persona (user experience).* [online] Available at: <**https://en.wikipedia.org/wiki/Persona#In_user_experience_design**>

58 Aspect, 2014. *Know your customer service persona.* [online] Available at: <**http://www.aspect.com/customer-service-personas**>

SECTION 4

1 Ratcliff, C., 2014. *Marketers more focused on acquisition than retention.* [online] Econsultancy. Available at: <**https://econsultancy.com/blog/65339-marketers-more-focused-on-acquisition-than-retention/**>

2 Lemmens, A. and Gupta, S., 2013. *Managing churn to maximise profits.* [online] Harvard Business School. Available at: <**http://hbswk.hbs.edu/item/7350.html**>

3 Pitney Bowes. *Pitney Bowes' latest press releases, articles and case studies, as well as archived information.* [online] Available at: <**http://pressroom.pitneybowes.co.uk/preventing-customer-churn/**>

4 Thompson, B., 2005. *The loyalty connection: secrets to customer retention and increased profits.* [pdf] Available at: <**http://www.ianbrooks. com/useful-ideas/articles_whitepapers/The Loyalty Connection.pdf**>

5 Swinscoe, A., 2014. *Customer engagement and lessons from the Scottish poet, Robert Burns – interview with Jamie Anderson of SAP.* [online] Available at: <**http://www.adrianswinscoe.com/ customer-engagement-and-lessons-from-the-scottish-poet-robert-burns- interview-with-jamie-anderson-of-sap/**>

6 Burns, R., 1786. 'To a louse.' [online] Burns Country. Available at: <**http://www.robertburns.org/works/97.shtml**>

7 Wikipedia. *Confirmation bias.* [online] Available at: <**https:// en.wikipedia.org/wiki/Confirmation_bias**>

8 Retail Gazette, 2013. Loyalty versus loyalty schemes – the paradigm. [online] *Retail Gazette.* Available at: <**http://www.retailgazette.co.uk/ blog/2013/11/33031-loyalty-versus-loyalty-schemes-the-paradigm**>

9 Moth, D., 2011. *Loyalty schemes don't create loyal consumers, says Ipsos MORI.* [online] Econsultancy. Available at: <**https://econsultancy .com/blog/8554-consumers-want-discounts-and-special-treatment-in- return-for-loyalty**>

10 Swinscoe, A., 2013. *Customer service and customer loyalty can be improved by using decision science – interview with Phil Barden.* [online] Available at: <**http://www.adrianswinscoe.com/ customer-service-and-customer-loyalty-can-be-improved-by-using- decision-science-interview-with-phil-barden/**>

11 Nunes, J. C. and Drèze, X., 2006. The endowed progress effect: how artificial advancement increases effort. *Journal of Consumer Research.* [pdf] Available at: <**http://papers.ssrn.com/sol3/papers. cfm?abstract_id=991962**>

12 Shaukat, T. and Auerback, P., 2012. *Loyalty: is it really working for you?* [online] McKinsey & Company. Available at: <**http://www. mckinseyonmarketingandsales.com/loyalty-is-it-really-working-for-you**>

13 Pandora RD, 2012. *Best Job | P&G London 2012 Olympic Games Film.* Available at: <**https://www.youtube.com/watch?v=SVGIrs2K2ow**>

14 Delo, C., 2012. *P&G marketing chief touts role of Facebook, Yahoo in 'Thank you, Mom' campaign.* [online] AdvertisingAge. Available at: <**http://adage.com/article/ digital/p-g-s-pritchard-touts-digital-social-olympics-push/236590/**>

15 Godin, S., 2010. *Loyalty.* [online] Available at: <**http://sethgodin
    .typepad.com/seths_blog/2010/09/loyalty.html**>

16 Swinscoe, A., 2014. *What drives customer loyalty – interview with Steve
    Sims of Badgeville.* [online] Available at: <**http://www.adrianswinscoe.com/
    what-drives-customer-loyalty-interview-with-steve-sims-of-badgeville/**>

17 Wikipedia. *Service recovery paradox.* [online] Available at: <**http://
    en.wikipedia.org/wiki/Service_recoverydox**>

18 de Matos, C. A., Henrique, J. L. and Rossi, C. A. V., 2007. Service
    recovery paradox: a meta-analysis. *Journal of Service Research.*
    [online] Available at: <**http://jsr.sagepub.com/content/10/1/60.abstract**>;
    and Magnini, V. P., Ford, J. B., Markowski, E. P. and Honeycutt
    Jr, E. D., 2007. *The service recovery paradox: justifiable theory or
    smoldering myth?* [pdf] Available at: <**http://www.emeraldinsight.com/
    journals.htm?articleid=1610308&show=pdf**>

19 Lammore. [online] Available at: <**http://www.lammore.co.uk/**>

20 ClickFox, 2012. *2012 brand loyalty survey.* [pdf] Available at:
    <**http://web.clickfox.com/rs/clickfox/images/cf-survey-results-brand-
    loyalty.pdf**>

21 Swinscoe, A., 2013. *Employee engagement is a commitment not a
    campaign – interview with Stan Phelps.* [online] Available at: <**http://
    www.adrianswinscoe.com/employee-engagement-is-a-commitment-not-
    a-campaign-interview-with-stan-phelps/**>

SECTION 5

1 Hinge, 2015. *2015 Professional Services Marketing Priorities.*
   [online] Available at: <**http://www.hingemarketing.com/library/
   article/2015-professional-services-marketing-priorities**>

2 Sirinides, M., 2014. *Most advisory firms don't have a strategy
   of landing client referrals.* [online] InvestmentNews. Available at:
   <**http://www.investmentnews.com/article/20141215/BLOG18/141219955/
   most-advisory-firms-dont-have-a-strategy-for-landing-client-referrals**>

3 Swinscoe, A., 2014. *How we built a community of customer
   advocates – interview with Joan Babinski of Brainshark.* [online]
   Available at: <**http://www.adrianswinscoe.com/how-we-built-a-community-
   of-customer-advocates-interview-with-joan-babinski-of-brainshark/**>

SECTION 6

1 Swinscoe, A., 2015. *Customer feedback is the most effective way of improving the financial performance of a business – interview with Guy Letts of CustomerSure.* [online] Available at: <**http://www .adrianswinscoe.com/customer-feedback-is-the-most-effective-way-of-improving-the-financial-performance-of-a-business-interview-with-guy-letts-of-customersure/**>

2 OpinionLab. *So long surveys! Opt-in is taking over.* [online] Available at: <**http://www.opinionlab.com/so-long-surveys/**>

3 Customer Champions. *Creating a customer-orientated culture.* [online] Available at: <**http://www.customerchampions.co.uk/creating-a-customer-orientated-culture/**>

4 Swinscoe, A., 2015. *Customer feedback is the most effective way of improving the financial performance of a business – interview with Guy Letts of CustomerSure.* [online] Available at: <**http://www. adrianswinscoe.com/customer-feedback-is-the-most-effective-way-of-improving-the-financial-performance-of-a-business-interview-with-guy-letts-of-customersure/**>

5 Swinscoe, A., 2014. *Improve customer experience by surveying your customers quickly – interview with Mark Smith of ContactEngine.* [online] Available at: <**http://www.adrianswinscoe.com/improve-customer-experience-by-surveying-your-customers-quicker-interview-with-mark-smith-of-contactengine/**>

6 Aberdeen Group. *Customer engagement analytics: how to use data to create (and keep) happy customers.* [online] Available at: <**http://v1.aberdeen.com/launch/report/research_report/9251-RR-Customer-Analytics.asp**>

7 Minkara, O., 2014. Misinterpreting customer data: good data can't save bad marketing. [online] *CMO Essentials.* Available at: <**http://cmoessentials.com/misinterpreting-customer-data-good-data-cant-save-bad-marketing/**>

8 Rankin, J., 2015. WPP launches bid for data company that devised Tesco clubcard. [online] *The Guardian.* Available at: <**http://www.theguardian.com/business/2015/mar/16/wpp-launch-bid-company-tesco-clubcard**>

9 Swinscoe, A., 2014. *Customer insight, big data and the bigger skill gap – interview with Vivek Jetley of EXL*. [online] Available at: <**http:// www.adrianswinscoe.com/customer-insight-big-data-and-the-bigger-skills-gap-interview-with-vivek-jetley-of-exl/**>

SECTION 7

1 Drucker Institute. *Peter Drucker's life and legacy*. [online] Available at: <**http://www.druckerinstitute.com/peter-druckers-life-and-legacy/**>

2 O'Connell, D., 2015. The Sunday Times Best 100 Companies. [online] *The Sunday Times*. Available at: <**http://appointments .thesundaytimes.co.uk/article/best100companies/**>

3 Swinscoe, A., 2013. *Our customer service and success is driven by happy people all striving for the same high standards – interview with Will Beckett of Hawksmoor*. [online] Available at: <**http://www .adrianswinscoe.com/our-customer-service-and-success-is-driven-by-happy-people-all-striving-for-the-same-high-standards-interview-with-will-beckett-of-hawksmoor/**>

4 Swinscoe, A., 2014. *An organisation constitution improves employee engagement and customer experience – interview with Chris Edmonds*. [online] Available at: <**http://www.adrianswinscoe. com/an-organisational-constitution-improves-employee-engagment-and-customer-experience-interview-with-chris-edmonds/**>

5 Crabtree, S., 2013. *Worldwide, 13% of employees are engaged at work*. [online] Gallup. Available at: <**http://www.gallup.com/ poll/165269/worldwide-employees-engaged-work.aspx**>

6 Gallup. *The culture of an engaged workplace – Q12 employee engagement*. [online] Available at: <**http://www.gallup.com/ services/169328/q12-employee-engagement.aspx**>

7 Customer Experience Matters, 2015. *Report: employee engagement benchmark study, 2015*. [online] Available at: <**https://experiencematters.wordpress.com/2015/02/17/ report-employee-engagement-benchmark-study-2015/**>

8 Swinscoe, A., 2013. *Employee engagement and what it takes to be the best – interview with Ryan Cheyne of Pets at Home*. [online] Available at: <**http://www.adrianswinscoe.com/ employee-engagement-and-what-it-takes-to-be-the-best-interview-with-ryan-cheyne-of-pets-at-home/**>

9   Heskett, J. L., Earl Sasser Jnr, W. and Schlesinger, L. A., 1997. *The service profit chain: how leading companies link profit and growth to loyalty, satisfaction and value.* The Free Press: New York.

10 Beck, R. and Harter, J., 2015. *Managers account for 70% of variance in employee engagement.* [online] Available at: <**http:// www.gallup.com/businessjournal/182792/managers-account-variance-employee-engagement.aspx**>

11 Swinscoe, A., 2012. *Employee engagement is not something that is done to employees – interview with Kevin Kruse.* [online] Available at: <**http://www.adrianswinscoe.com/employee-engagement-is-not-something-that-is-done-to-employees-interview-with-kevin-kruse/**>

12 Karsan, R. and Kruse, K., 2011. *We: how to increase performance and profits through full engagement.* John Wiley & Sons: Hoboken, NJ; and Kruse, K., 2012. *Employee engagement 2.0: how to motivate your team for high performance.* The Kruse Group: Richboro, PA.

13 Swinscoe, A., 2011. *Customer experience, back to basics and creating a customer focused business – interview with Syed Hasan of Responsetek.* [online] Available at: <**http://www.adrianswinscoe .com/customer-experience-back-to-basics-and-creating-a-customer-focused-business-interview-with-syed-hasan-of-responsetek/**>

14 Robinson, D. Perryman, S. and Hayday, S., 2004. *The drivers of employee engagement.* [online] Institute for Employment Studies. Available at: <**http://www.employment-studies.co.uk/report-summary-drivers-employee-engagement?id=408**> and <**http://www.scarlettsurveys .com/employee-surveys/drivers-of-employee-engagement**>

15 IT-Online, 2015. *Gap between customer, employee experience.* [online] Available at: <**http://it-online.co.za/2015/06/23/gap-between-customer-employee-experience/**>

16 Swinscoe, A., 2015. *The pre-life, early life and in-life stages of the employee experience – interview with Jo Taylor.* [online] Available at: <**http://www.adrianswinscoe.com/the-pre-life-early-life-and-in-life-stages-of-the-employee-experience-interview-with-jo-taylor/**>

17 Stewart, H., 2012. *The happy manifesto: make your organization a great workplace.* Kogan Page: London.

18 Swinscoe, A., 2012. *Create an enjoyable customer experience and get a Net Promotor Score of 70%.* [online] Available at: <**http://www**

.adrianswinscoe.com/create-an-enjoyable-customer-experience-and-get-a-net-promoter-score-of-70/>

SECTION 8

1 Zappo Insights. *Holacracy and self-organization.* [online] Available at: <**http://www.zapposinsights.com/about/holacracy**> and <**http://www.holacracy.org/**>

2 Gore. *A team-based, flat lattice organization.* [online] Available at: <**http://www.gore.com/en_xx/aboutus/culture/**>

3 Best Companies. *W L Gore & Associates.* [online] Available at: <**http://www.b.co.uk/Company/Profile/305950**>

4 Gore, 2015. *W. L. Gore & Associates named on the 2015 Fortune 100 best companies to work for list.* [online] Available at: <**http://www.gore.com/en_xx/news/FORTUNE-100-best-2015.html**> and <**http://www.gore.com/en_gb/news/sunday_2014.html**>

5 WorldBlu. *10 principles of organizational democracy.* [online] Available at: <**http://www.worldblu.com/democratic-design/principles.php**> and <**http://www.worldblu.com/awardee-profiles/2015.php**>

6 WD-40, 2015. *WD-40 company: corporate overview.* [pdf] Available at: <**http://investor.wd40company.com/files/doc_presentations/2015/070815-WDFC-Corporate-Overview-FINAL.pdf**>

7 Swinscoe, A., 2014. *Looptail and changing the world through fully engaged employees and customers – interview with Bruce Poon Tip.* [online] Available at: <**http://www.adrianswinscoe.com/looptail-and-changing-the-world-through-fully-engaged-employees-and-customers-interview-with-bruce-poon-tip/**>

8 Poon Tip, B., 2013. *Looptail: how one company changed the world by reinventing business.* Business Plus: New York

9 Swinscoe, A., 2014. *Five ways to become more agile and responsive to your customers' needs.* [online] Available at: <**http://www.adrianswinscoe.com/five-ways-to-become-more-agile-and-responsive-to-your-customers-needs/**>

10 Swinscoe, A., 2014. *Business needs to be agile and customer centric if it is to avoid the coming customerpocalypse – interview with Alan Trefler, CEO of Pegasystems.* [online] Available at: <**http://www.adrianswinscoe.com/**

business-needs-to-be-agile-and-customer-centric-if-it-is-to-avoid-
the-coming-customerpocalypse-interview-with-alan-trefler-ceo-of-
pegasystems/>

11 Bill, G., Sims, P., McLean, A. N. and Mayer, D., 2007. *Discovering
your authentic leadership.* [online] *Harvard Business Review.* Available
at: <**https://hbr.org/2007/02/discovering-your-authentic-leadership/ar/1**>

12 Swinscoe, A., 2012. *Using systems thinking to improve
customer satisfaction and employee engagement – interview
with Rob Brown of Aviva.* [online] Available at: <**http://www
.adrianswinscoe.com/using-systems-thinking-to-improve-customer-
satisfaction-and-employee-engagement-interview-with-rob-brown-of-
aviva/**>

13 Vanguard. [online] Available at: <**http://vanguard-method.net/**>

14 Swinscoe, A., 2013. *Systems thinking, customer service and
unlearning the way we do things – interview with John Seddon of
Vanguard.* [online] Available at: <**http://www.adrianswinscoe.com/
systems-thinking-customer-service-and-unlearning-the-way-we-do-
things-interview-with-john-seddon-of-vanguard/**>

15 IBE, 2014. *Business Ethics Briefing.* [pdf] Available at: <**https://www
.ibe.org.uk/userassets/briefings/b39_customers.pdf**>

16 Tovey, A., 2015. 'People would rather go to the dentist than
a car dealer – we've got to end that.' [online] *The Telegraph.*
Available at: <**http://www.telegraph.co.uk/finance/newsbysector/
retailandconsumer/11800921/SUNDAY-People-would-rather-go-to-the-
dentist-than-a-car-dealer-weve-got-to-end-that.html**>

17 Swinscoe, A., 2015. *How we transferred our organisation and
our customer experience – interview with Damian Thompson of
Principality Building Society.* [online] Available at: <**http://www
.adrianswinscoe.com/how-we-transformed-our-organisation-and-our-
customer-experience-interview-with-damian-thompson-of-principality-
building-society/**>

18 Thodey, D., 2014. *Why everybody should think they are the Chief
Customer Officer – reflections on building a customer focused
business.* [online] LinkedIn. Available at: <**https://www.linkedin.com/
pulse/20140522060750-130682857-why-everybody-should-think-they-
are-the-chief-customer-officer-reflections-on-building-a-customer-
focused-business**>

19 BusinessManagement, 2013. *CEO's duty: customer service rep?* [online] Available at: <**http://www.businessmanagementdaily.com/34056/ceos-duty-customer-service-rep**>

20 Swinscoe, A., 2014. *Social leadership and why the C-Suite has to go social – interview with Ted Coiné and Mark Babbitt.* [online] Available at: <**http://www.adrianswinscoe.com/social-leadership-and-why-the-c-suite-has-to-go-social-interview-with-ted-coine-and-mark-babbitt/**>

21 Kitching, C., 2014. EXCLUSIVE: No more Mr Meanie! Ryanair's famously combative boss Michael O'Leary admits he was too extreme and should have been 'nicer' to customers sooner. [online] *Mail Online*. Available at: <**http://www.dailymail.co.uk/travel/travel_news/article-2813863/Controversial-Ryanair-boss-admits-no-frills-carrier-nicer-customers-sooner.html**>

22 Swinscoe, A., 2015. *A degree of humility always succeeds in business – interview with Michael O'Leary of Ryanair.* [online] Available at: <**http://www.adrianswinscoe.com/a-degree-of-humility-always-succeeds-in-business-interview-with-michael-oleary-of-ryanair/**>

23 Heidreck & Struggles. *The CEO report: Embracing the paradoxes of leadership and the power of doubt.* [pdf] Available at: <**http://www.heidrick.com/Knowledge-Center/Publication/The-CEO-Report**>

24 Wikipedia. *Goodhart's Law.* [online] Available at: <**https://en.wikipedia.org/wiki/Goodhart's_law**>

25 Bazerman, M. H. and Tenbrunsel, A. E., 2011. Ethical breakdowns. [online] *Harvard Business Review.* Available at: <**https://hbr.org/2011/04/ethical-breakdowns**>

26 Verrill, A., 2012. *A Zappos lesson in customer service metrics.* [online] Customer Service Investigator. Available at: <**http://csi.softwareadvice.com/a-zappos-lesson-in-customer-service-metrics-1101029/**>; and Michelli, J., 2011. *The Zappos experience: 5 principles to inspire, engage and WOW.* McGraw-Hill: New York.

27 Hsieh, T., 2010. *Why I sold Zappos.* [online] Inc. Available at: <**http://www.inc.com/magazine/20100601/why-i-sold-zappos.html**>

28 Swinscoe, A., 2010. *Culture and values can be a great base for growth. For some it's everything.* [online] Available at: <**http://www.adrianswinscoe.com/culture-great-base-growth/**>

29 Bezos, J., 2009. *Video from Jeff Bezos about Amazon and Zappos.* [video online] Available at: <**https://www.youtube.com/**

watch?v=-hxX_Q5CnaA>; and Parr, B., 2009. *Here's why Amazon bought Zappos.* [online] Mashable. Available at: <**http://mashable. com/2009/07/22/amazon-bought-zappos/**>

30 Lam, B., 2014. *The wasted workday.* [online] The Atlantic. Available at: <**http://www.theatlantic.com/business/archive/2014/12/the-wasted- workday/383380/**>; and Workfront. *Latest study reveals companies are failing employees.* [online] Available at: <**http://www.workfront .com/enterprise/resource/whitepaper/state-enterprise-work**>

31 Swinscoe, A., 2013. *Employee engagement is like rolling a snowball uphill – interview with Peter A. Hunter.* [online] Available at: <**http:// www.adrianswinscoe.com/employee-engagement-is-like-rolling-a- snowball-uphill-interview-with-peter-a-hunter/**>

32 Gartner, 2015. *Gartner's 2015 hype cycle for emerging technologies identifies the computing innovations that organizations should monitor.* [online] Available at: <**http://www.gartner.com/newsroom/ id/3114217**>

33 Fenn, J., 2014. *Applying lessons from 20 years of hype cycles to your own innovation and forecasting strategies.* [online] Gartner. Available at: <**https://www.gartner.com/doc/2847417?**>

INDEX